[Between the Words]

"I strongly encourage you to read this book on listening. It will enable you to be more like Christ and sharpen your interpersonal skills."

Dr. Neil T. Anderson, founder and president emeritus, Freedom In Christ Ministries

"Dr. Wakefield has prescribed the purpose and process of clarifying the messages we receive for effective and caring response."

Naomi Rhode, CSP CPAE Speaker Hall of Fame; past president, National Speakers Association

"What a winner! Norm's style of using illustrations from his own life experiences and providing practical 'reflect and apply' activities makes this a wonderful resource to help others individually, as well as a practical discussion guide in a group setting. After giving specific insights to encourage others, Norm moves the reader along to deal with his/her own personal growth through listening. This book provides the needed tools to become a powerful, perceptive listener. I am looking forward to the publication of *Between the Words: The Art of Perceptive Listening* for personal growth and to give away to those I mentor and teach."

Dr. Ruth Ann Breuninger, Executive Director, Invest in a Life

"If you want to bring strength and hope to your relationships, read and practice *Between the Words.* Dr. Wakefield refocuses our attention on one of the most overlooked, yet powerful disciplines in the culture today."

Dr. Bruce McNicol, coauthor of bestseller, *The Ascent of a Leader*; president, Leadership Catalyst

[Between the Words]

THE ART OF PERCEPTIVE LISTENING

Dr. Norm Wakefield

Fleming H. Revell
A Division of Baker Book House Co
Grand Rapids, Michigan 49516

Published by Fleming H. Revell
a division of Baker Book House Company
P.O. Box 6287, Grand Rapids, MI 49516-6287

Printed in the United States of America

Library of Congress Cataloging-in-Publication Data

Wakefield, Norm.
    Between the words : the art of perceptive listening / Norm Wakefield.
        p.   cm.
    Includes bibliographical references.
    ISBN 0-8007-5806-4 (pbk.)
      1. Listening—Religious aspects—Christianity. 2. Interpersonal relations—Religious aspects—Christianity. 3.Christian life. I. Title.
BV4647.L56 .W35 2002
248.4—dc21
                                    20020021635

Between the Words is another creative resource from the authors at Nappaland Communications Inc. To contact a Nappaland author, access the free webzine for families at: www.Nappaland.com

For current information about all releases from Baker Book House, visit our web site:
                  http://www.bakerbooks.com

This book came about because of the persistent work of my son-in-law, Mike Nappa. Mike, you are a cherished friend, a cheerful encourager, a loving husband to Amy and a great dad to Tony. I joyfully honor you and your diligence in making this book a reality.

[Contents]

•

[Introduction]

•

I met Benida Madill shortly after our family moved to Phoenix, Arizona. She was in her early seventies, living in a cluttered mobile home on her government pension. Benida's "thorn in the flesh" was her deafness. She wore hearing aids in both ears, but even with the best the market could provide, she still couldn't hear much, including the high whistle and squeal her aids made when they were turned up too loud. When someone would ask her to turn them down, she'd get mad.

One day when we were chatting, Benida said, "My inability to hear makes life difficult. When I can't hear the conversations going on around me, I get annoyed and frustrated. I feel left out."

Benida wanted to listen, but she couldn't hear. She was a bright, articulate, and interesting person who felt robbed of one of her senses.

Through her I learned to cherish my ability *to hear* and have been motivated to become more than just a hearer, but a perceptive listener. By this I mean *to listen with discernment and compassion.* God has taught me that others have wonderful insights and life experiences that enrich my life if I listen carefully and learn how to "read between the lines."

Most of my life has been spent in teaching, pastoring, and counseling people. My ability to listen perceptively is central to maintaining and building healthy interpersonal relationships. When I slow down, clear my mind, and begin to hear the hearts of those around me, the potential for significant relationships to develop increases dramatically. Many have told me that my commitment to listen to them has been a source of encouragement and help.

Another reason I am so committed to being a perceptive listener is because I have discovered that our Lord is an active listener. He hears the cry of the brokenhearted. He listens to our prayers. He rejoices when we sing songs of praise and adoration to him. One way to reflect his image is to become an effective, perceptive listener too. If listening is important to my Lord, it must be important for me.

The book you hold in your hands reflects my commitment to learn all I could about listening. Most of it is the distillation of reading, observation, and life experiences. My goal is to make the subject as readable and user-friendly as possible. Above all I want to help you become a better listener. If you do, I am convinced that your life will be more fruitful, and you will have a positive impact on those around you. My prayer is that your family members, friends, and work associates' lives will be blessed by your listening ear.

CHAPTER ONE

[Help! I'm In over My Head]

●

It is impossible to over-emphasize the immense need
men have to be really listened to, to be taken seriously,
to be understood.[1]

Paul Tournier

A fool thinks he needs no advice, but a wise man listens
to others.

Proverbs 12:15 TLB

There lived a young ruler who was suddenly propelled
into national leadership when his father died. It wasn't

11

that he was taken off guard. His dad had often said, "Someday this task will be yours. You'll carry the future well-being of our nation on your shoulders. I'll do the best I can to get you ready, but when the day comes, the ball will be in your court."

His new responsibilities presented him with several difficult decisions. For starters, how would he unify the nation now that his father was gone? Troublemakers and opportunists would see the former ruler's death as an excuse to create dissension. What could he do to get ready for these new burdens?

One great resource the young leader had was a strong confidence in the living God. He decided to get away for a few days to a favorite hideaway for prayer and meditation.

As he turned off the highway and drove up the tree-lined entry, he thought, "It's good to be here."

After he settled in, he took a walk along some of his favorite pathways, immersing himself in the beauty and solitude of everything around him. He was reminded of how much he'd hungered for time alone with God. "Lord, I need this time with you," he prayed, "time to open my heart to you, time for you to refresh and renew me, time to let you strengthen and counsel me. Lord, how much I need your peace and presence."

After dinner the young ruler went to his room. As he unwound, a sense of personal peace and physical comfort overtook him. He fell asleep. He dreamed. The Lord appeared before him in his awesome splendor. The sense of his presence made the young ruler tremble.

His Lord spoke: "I know your desire to honor me and serve the people you lead. Now ask for whatever you want me to give to you."

Ask for whatever he wanted? The young ruler was not prepared to answer such a question. All sorts of thoughts flashed through his mind. The most powerful country on earth? Riches beyond measure: gold, silver, precious jewels? Power to control men, yes, even to do miracles? Long life with perfect health?

But these first thoughts were swept aside as another one overpowered them. An inner, persistent voice called out, "Wisdom to be an effective leader of your nation." Wisdom? But he already had a good mind. Lots of people had told him that he was a man of wisdom. And in these early months of ruling, he'd demonstrated that he had what it took.

•

"Give your servant a listening heart to provide wise, effective leadership."

•

Still . . . his job required much discernment when people came to him with complex issues. Even with the keen mind and insight he possessed, he often felt the pressure of decisions that had to be made.

Finally, the young ruler responded, "Lord, you've thrust me into this demanding place. But I'm only a young man—sometimes I feel like a child. At times I feel overwhelmed and scared to make decisions that affect so many people. The responsibility for this nation is crushing.

"So here's my request: give your servant a listening heart to provide wise, effective leadership. Yes, a *listening heart*. I need a God-given capacity to hear with the heart, to be able to separate right from wrong, to be able to make accurate decisions. That's it, dear Lord. This is what I want most of all—the supernatural ability to listen from the heart."

The Lord smiled.

He was glad that the young ruler had chosen something infinitely more valuable than long life, wealth, or international supremacy. He spoke, "I will grant what you have asked. I will give you a wise and listening heart. There will never be another man like you. No person will ever be as competent to hear with the inner ear. Listen and you will be a wise and just leader."

Then the young leader awoke.

Did you recognize the young leader I've been describing? I drew this story from the biblical account of King Solomon's early years as king of Israel. Did you know that Solomon's famous request was to be a skilled *listener*? Most translations use the words *understanding* or *discerning*, but the Hebrew word literally means "hearing." Solomon recognized that to be an effective leader, he needed to be an effective listener.

Is Listening Really That Important?

I read a true account of a man who was anticipating the sale of his company. He had decided on a figure of $3 million as the asking price. When he sat down to negotiate the sale, he felt an inner compulsion to remain silent. The investors opened the discussion giving their appraisal of the company—what they saw as its strengths and weaknesses. Finally their spokesman came to the point. He said, "We'll give you $3.5 million and not a penny more." At the end of the negotiations a sum of $3.65 million was agreed on. The seller's commitment to listen had earned him $650,000.

His decision to remain silent had come as the result of training he had received. He had remembered a statement: "The better you listen, the more you learn about how the customer feels about your product."

In his autobiography Lee Iacocca says, "I only wish I could find an institute that teaches people how to listen. After all, a good manager needs to listen at least as much as he needs to talk. Too many people fail to realize that good communication goes in both directions."[2]

Numerous research studies consistently demonstrate that listening is one of the most crucial skills that employees need in the workplace.

A study was undertaken at a major university to determine the qualities and behaviors that young people looked for in their leaders. These could be either peers or adults. Listening was found to be the most important behavior that adolescents desired in their leaders. Followers want leaders who listen to them.[3]

> •
>
> A good manager needs to listen at least as much as he needs to talk.
>
> •

Studies that go back as far as 1929 demonstrate that listening occupies between 45 and 53 percent of our communication activity—far more than speaking, writing, or reading. Studies of executives' activities reveal similar results. They spend between 45 and 63 percent of their day listening. Think of it! During a typical day most of us spend hours involved in listening. Doesn't it make sense to become as skilled a listener as possible?

The World's Best Listener

Another reason listening is important is because it's one of God's attributes.

It is possible when reading the Bible to overlook something significant. I've discovered that I may have read a passage several times and then when I read it again, a word or phrase jumps out at me that I'd never noticed before. Sometimes this occurs because we have been conditioned to see things through preconceived "filters" that inhibit our seeing all that there is to be seen. For example, the God I was presented with during my early Christian years could best be described as a stainless-steel God. Nothing could penetrate him. Feelings or emotions couldn't touch him because that would make him imperfect.

Thankfully, through persistent study of the Bible and helpful Christian literature, I've come to a more dramatic and wholesome view of our Lord. I've become more amazed daily at his warm, tender heart.

God Listens

Think about this amazing truth—God listens to you. Ponder that a moment. Isn't it incredible! The sovereign Lord of the universe *listens* to you and to me. What a down-to-earth expression of his amazing grace! I know that this is true because the Bible clearly states it. Our Lord *hears* his people.

Our Lord listens for the cry of a needy child. Abraham was a great man of God whose life is recorded in the Old Testament. He had two sons, Isaac, the son the Lord promised through his wife, Sarah, and Ishmael, the son of Sarah's servant, Hagar. When Sarah became jealous of Hagar and Ishmael, she had Abraham send Hagar away with the child. The two wandered about in the desert until their water and food supplies were exhausted. In this pitiful condition, mother and son began to weep in despair. Let's listen to what Scripture says:

> God heard the boy crying, and the angel of God called to Hagar from heaven and said to her, "What is the matter, Hagar? Do not be afraid; God has heard the boy crying as he lies there. Lift the boy up and take him by the hand, for I will make him into a great nation."
>
> Genesis 21:17–18

Isn't that incredible? Our God's hearing is so sensitive that he immediately tunes in to the cry of young children. This profound thought challenges me as a parent and teacher. If God takes time to listen to children, I too want to listen.

Our Lord listens to the cry of a brokenhearted wife. Hannah desperately wanted a child. Her husband, Elkanah, was a compassionate man, but he had another wife who bore children, and she delighted in reminding Hannah that she was childless—a stigma of inferiority in biblical times. Though Elkanah listened to Hannah, it was hard for him to comprehend the great longing that built up in his wife's heart (1 Sam. 1:1–8).

So Hannah exposed her aching heart to the Lord in prayer. His ever-listening ear heard her lament clearly and with empathy. The Bible says that he acted on her behalf, and Samuel was born to Hannah. If you are a woman, let Hannah remind you of One who is always near, bending his ear to listen for you and to you.

Our Lord hears the cry of a troubled man. The writer of Psalm 116 voices his profound gratitude to the Lord for his listening ear. Listen to the psalmist's eager testimony:

I love the LORD, because He hears my voice and my supplications. Because He has inclined His ear to me, therefore I shall call upon Him as long as I live.

Psalm 116:1–2 NASB

David might well have written this psalm. We know that he had experienced many frightening and painful events that sometimes left him despondent, anxious, and sorrowful. We can only imagine what circumstances he may have faced. But in the midst of these distressing situations, he knows that when he cries out, "O Lord, I beseech Thee, save my life!" there is One whose ear is always bent to listen.

Notice the response of one who knows that he has the Lord's ear. "I shall call upon Him as long as I live." The writer is deeply grateful that there is someone who cares enough to listen. We all value people who love us enough to listen to us. The psalmist's words remind us of the awesome power of a listening ear. The wise and discerning listener endears himself to our heart, fostering a strong relational bond.

The listening God theme reoccurs throughout the Bible. It is a central element of David's psalms. He repeatedly acknowledges that the Lord heard him as he cried out. David's distress is evident in Psalm 6. He uses phrases such as "my bones are in agony" (v. 2), "my soul is in anguish" (v. 3), "I am worn out from groaning; all night long I flood my bed with weeping and drench my couch in tears" (v. 6). In verses 8 and 9 he declares his confidence that "the LORD has heard my weeping. The LORD has heard my cry for mercy."

Our Lord listens to the cry of an oppressed people. God listens to his family members—you and me. He heard the Israelites as they groaned under the inhumane Egyptian bondage. "The Israelites groaned in their slavery and cried out. . . . God heard their groaning" (Exod. 2:23, 24). The heart of the God of kindness and mercy must have been deeply touched as he listened to his children weep in agony under the crushing load of tyranny.

Our Lord listens to his beloved Son. Even Jesus needed someone to listen to him. At the graveside of his friend Lazarus, Jesus raises his eyes to heaven and says:

> Father, I thank you that you have heard me. And I knew that you always hear me, but I said this for the benefit of the people standing here, that they may believe that you sent me.
>
> John 11:41–42

During his earthly ministry Jesus consistently displayed an ongoing communion between Father and Son. This would be meaningless unless our Father was present and listening to him. It's especially obvious in John's Gospel. A careful reading reveals Jesus' delight in the intimacy between him and his Father. One relevant implication of this truth concerns Jesus' present ministry. He is seated at the right hand of the Father, interceding for you and me (Heb. 4:14–16). If our heavenly Father were preoccupied and not listening to the Lord Jesus, Jesus' intercession on our behalf would be pointless. But we know that he is quick to hear both the Son, in whom he delights, and his children, whom the Son represents.

Jesus Listens

Our heavenly Father's perceptive spirit is revealed in the heart of the Lord Jesus. He clearly demonstrates God's compassionate, listening heart. During his earthly visit he attracted multitudes, not merely by what he said, but equally by his willingness to listen to the individual's distressing circumstances. After hearing the full message, he would respond with the appropriate word or touch. Jesus listens (Matt. 8:2–3; 9:27–29; Luke 7:11–15).

Jesus also expressed the full meaning of listening. Because he could hear the full message, he could always respond appropriately. Frequently, we meet people who do not listen effectively and who thus respond incorrectly or not at all. Not so with Jesus. His response is always appropriate because he knows every detail, emotion, or circumstance of every situation.

Why Listening Is Important

At this point you may be saying, "I've always known that God can hear. What's so special about that?" I'd say it's special for several reasons.

Reason number one: Listening brings God joy. Our loving Lord finds joy in listening to his creation—and especially the crown of his creation, man. Aren't you thankful that God didn't create man and then leave him to fend for himself? Rather, our God became vitally involved in our lives, actively communicating with us.

Reason number two: Listening fills my need. The fact that my God listens tells me that he recognizes my basic need for attention. All of us cry out to be listened to (I recognize that some of us adapted to life when no one was listening, so we live as though no one cared). God knew we would have that need; it appears to be basic to our nature. We were not created to live in isolation.

Reason number three: Listening is a way to show God's love to others. God gives dignity to the act of listening. He demonstrates from his life that it is an act of love. He makes it of special significance—an important ministry in and of itself. In our relationships with both Christians and non-Christians, we have the happy privilege of exemplifying this exciting aspect of our Father's nature—that he cares enough to listen.

Perceptive Listening—It's the Real Thing

If listening is so important, then we must do all we can to develop this attribute of God in ourselves.

To some extent everyone listens. Even a deaf person listens with his eyes and his sense of touch. But because listening can occur on several levels, it is wise to think of the act of listening as being on a continuum from weak and ineffective to powerful and *perceptive*. Keep these two facts in mind. First, each of us has one style of listening with which we are most comfortable. In other words, we place ourselves somewhere on the continuum that is typical of most of our relationships.

ineffective	perceptive
unskilled	skilled
unmotivated	motivated
listener	listener

And here's a second significant fact. Each of us can shift where we are on the continuum depending on the following:

- where we are
- whom we are with
- the circumstances we are encountering
- our physical/emotional condition

Our effectiveness as listeners fluctuates according to a variety of factors, which we can often do something about. This increases our ability to hear.

For the remainder of this book, I would like you to think of listening in a special way. Rather than using the single word "listening" I'd like you to get used to the term, *perceptive listening.* To help distinguish it from other kinds of listening, let's look at the five kinds of listening.

1. You can listen for the *words* that another is speaking.
2. You can listen for the *words* and watch for *non-verbal clues.*
3. You can listen to discover the *meanings* within the person's message.
4. You can listen to identify the *defined or undefined emotions* embodied in the message.
5. You can listen to discern *the message that is behind the verbal and nonverbal communication.*

I am not suggesting that we will have the time, capacity, or energy to listen in the most involved way to every

21

communication that comes our way. We are bombarded with hundreds of messages during an average day, and we have to practice some selectivity in what we listen to. Being a perceptive listener helps us better pick up clues that the unskilled listener misses. By doing this, we are better able to discern those situations which need the fullest level of perceptive listening and those which we judge to be less significant.

Here's how it works in my life. I'm married and have five adult children. Two married children live in the same city I do. I teach in a graduate school, and I have regular contacts with over fifty students (our student body is much larger than that). I am also committed to the mentoring process, and presently I have a number of students with whom I maintain mentor-protégé relationships. Then there are regular interactions with fellow professors. I am actively involved in my church—training, interacting, and shepherding, to name a few ways. On top of that, I receive phone calls, letters, and e-mails from all sorts of people.

> •
> I simply must be a perceptive listener to function well and be a loving, caring individual.
> •

It shouldn't be difficult for you to see why one of my most persistent and crucial tasks is to discern with whom I should be involved in a significant way. Whom should I listen to? And while I try to listen to everyone who speaks to me, I must make some judgments about which relationships are most needy, which information is most crucial, and so forth. *I simply must be a perceptive listener to function well and be a loving, caring individual.*

Now let's go back to our five kinds of listeners and look at the list in another way. It might be helpful for you to think of these as levels of listening. From that perspective each is built upon the preceding level. As

I move to a higher level, I become a more perceptive listener because I am getting more of the communication. In fact, in level five I may be hearing communication that the speaker isn't aware of or is not intending to communicate. The person may be so emotionally involved that she is incapable of recognizing all she is communicating, but because I am fully attuned to her, I am picking up lots of data that I can feed back. Thus she will become more aware of her own issues.

5. Meaning behind
4. Emotions
3. Meanings
2. Nonverbal
1. Words

If you look at the five steps as levels of listening, your *goal is to move to the highest level.* The highest level will incorporate all the preceding levels. As you work through the issues presented in this book, I encourage you to discover where your strengths and weaknesses lie. Then focus your energy on building greater skill at each level, but especially where you need greater strength.

How Will Listening Change You?

Perceptive listening will make you wiser. Plutarch said, "Know how to listen, and you will profit even from those who talk badly." I started this chapter by relating Solomon's plea for a deeper capacity to listen perceptively. We know the outcome of that request—Solomon became famous for his wisdom. Later he wrote, "Let the wise listen and add to their learning" (Prov. 1:5). He spoke about the blessing that comes to the person who listens for wisdom.

Perceptive listening will sensitize you to valuable input from others. You will pick up important data that others miss. That data will help you come to better conclusions or relate to others with greater discernment. It represents an active internal process that makes more information and insight available to the listener. An active, perceptive listener is more in touch with the environment, with people, events, and things. The first person to benefit from listening is the listener himself.

> •
>
> The first person
> to benefit
> from listening is the
> listener himself.
>
> •

Perceptive listening will allow you to build stronger interpersonal relationships. People tend to seek out the perceptive listener. This is especially true of the listener who demonstrates empathetic care for the speaker—or for the listener who is willing to actively engage with the person who has a problem.

For a number of years I have asked many individuals to describe the person who has most influenced his or her life. I discovered that a consistent pattern of characteristics emerged and that one recurring feature was listening. A person who influences another's life expresses an interest in that person and demonstrates a desire to hear about his ideas, activities, problems, and so on. The listener expresses a wish to have a two-way relationship.

Through the act of listening, we frequently pick up clues that someone else is seeking a relationship with us. I recall speaking at a conference some time ago on the subject of building interpersonal relationships. One of the participants, a girl in her teens, decided to practice one of the concepts I'd proposed on her dad. She went to him and expressed a desire for them to go out for lunch together. He made some excuse, so she tried another tactic. Still he didn't pick up the clues. Finally, his wife said to him, "Your daughter wants to work on her relationship with you. She's been trying to get a lunch date with you."

Later, the girl's father related this incident to me and commented on how much he needed to work on his listening skills so that he would not miss other opportunities. Every day people are seeking out individuals with whom they can relate. Listening skills are among our most important resources in furthering the relational process.

Perceptive listening will increase your impact on people's lives. One of my goals in writing this book was to get people excited about the potential of developing their perceptive-listening skills. I know individuals who are willing to pay high fees to seek the expertise of listening specialists; we call them counselors, therapists, psychologists, and psychiatrists. I am eager to help nonspecialists increase their listening skills, because I know the power of perceptive listening. It is a significant form of ministry available to anyone who is willing to cultivate this attitude and skill.

This truth was impressed on me a number of years ago when I read a report of telephone crisis help lines that reach out to individuals who are facing difficult and seemingly insurmountable problems. The author of the report discovered that the power of this help was not in what the "helpers" said, but in the way they listened. They were taught that the act of listening itself was a way of helping. The researcher also

> •
>
> I know individuals who are willing to pay high fees to seek the expertise of listening specialists; we call them counselors, therapists, psychologists, and psychiatrists.
>
> •

found that when a certain approach to listening was adopted, the callers were more able to help themselves.[4]

There is clear, convincing evidence supporting the fact that one of the most powerful ways we help others is through perceptive listening. And this kind of listening is within the grasp of anyone who will commit himself to cultivate healthy attitudes and skills that underlie it.

How Will It Help Others?

The perceptive listener touches others' lives in significant ways. People make comments like, "You've really helped me." "Thanks for being there for me." What makes perceptive listening so powerful? Here are five benefits the speaker gains when you and I practice perceptive listening:

Speakers are helped to express their feelings in a constructive manner. The frustrated, angry, discouraged, or frightened individual is usually looking for some means to process these emotions. Perceptive listening helps him talk out the emotions, feeding back what he hears. Through this ventilation process, the emotions are discharged constructively, and the troubled person is able to turn to healthy solutions.

Think of a troubled teen who has come home from school bottled up with anger. It has been a bad day all around. If only there were someone he could talk to, someone who would listen so the anger could be released. But both his parents are at work, and when they come home, they are too busy to listen.

Perceptive listening helps others talk out ideas, problems, and decisions that need resolving. Plato said, "Thinking is the talking of the soul with itself." The compassionate listener helps the individual think out loud. We are constantly faced with new information or decisions that we need to think through. Many times the simple act of talking out whatever is confronting us helps us sort out information, opinions, and conflicts.

I teach in a graduate school, speak at seminars, and write books. As I prepare new material I feel the need to have someone else listen as I process new thoughts, try to resolve some difficult problem, or rehearse what I want to present. I'll often seek out my wife, Winnie, and say, "Honey, would you listen to this? Does it make sense? I need your thoughts." Winnie's willingness to be a perceptive listener is an act of love to me.

Perceptive listening is one of the best means of expressing unselfish love (that's one reason it's so powerful). Listening says, "You are important," or "Your ideas, problems, and feelings are important to me. I care about you." Listening is a primary means of modeling God's love. Think of that! What potential for Christ's people to relate to one another in a practical way! We show others we love them by the way we listen to them.

> •
> We show others we love them by the way we listen to them.
> •

That's true for me. When I have something I feel the need to share, I deeply appreciate someone who will listen intently, expressing loving care. By contrast, the individual who constantly interrupts, changes the subject, or seems disinterested frustrates me—especially when I'm discouraged or excited and want so much to share my experience. Thank God, *he* always listens.

Perceptive listening provides the foundation for wise counsel. The godly wisdom of New Testament writer James reminds us that we are to "be quick to listen, slow to speak and slow to become angry" (James 1:19). Only by listening patiently and perceptively can we prepare ourselves to understand another's struggle adequately and to respond in a helping way. Quick advice frequently speaks to a false problem.

And here's the mega reason why I'm sold on the impact of perceptive listening. I've discovered that careful perceptive listening is often essential to finding the real source of the problem. Frequently, what a person *thinks* is his problem or need is not the real one at all, but only the felt or perceived one. As he talks it out with a perceptive listener, he begins to see other dimensions of which he was unaware and which greatly influence the solution.

> •
> Perceptive listening
> is often essential
> to finding
> the real source
> of the problem.
> •

Perceptive listening says, "I want to understand you. I want to know you." It is one of the most basic ways to convey a sense of respect, to treat another with dignity. Through this act we affirm to another person that God is willing to listen, that he eagerly waits for his troubled child to come to him and discover the compassion and deep concern of his loving Father.

I have a friend who is a young girl. She knows that she can always go to her dad when she is having problems with her boyfriend. Her dad will put his arm around her and simply say, "Tell me about it." What a comfort to know he's there to listen.

Unquestionably, the listening I have been speaking about is a powerful way to say, "I love you." Such listening embodies something of the nature of God himself. It makes available to the Holy Spirit a channel through which to communicate love and a helpful, appropriate response. This power to impact others is available to anyone in God's family who longs to be available to his fellow family members.

Power of Listening

Perceptive listening pays big dividends. You may not have the charisma to attract crowds, or the intellectual depth to impress people with your brilliance. You may lack the skill to write a best-seller, but you can cultivate a power that will impact both your own life and the lives of others around you. Like Solomon, you can become a discerning, sensitive listener. You can learn to listen using eyes and ears, mind and heart. Why not invest some of your time and energy to become a pro at it? It will make you rich in many ways. In the following chapters, I'll show you how.

Time to Reflect and Apply

Perceptive listening is a commitment to others, an attitude of serving, and a package of skills that can be developed. If you are to profit from what you read, you must take additional steps. I want to begin by asking you to do some self-evaluation. The more you follow through with the application exercises, the greater the chances that you will become more perceptive.

The following response guide will help you evaluate your listening attitude and skills. After completing the evaluation, consider asking a family member or close friend to share his or her perspective on the kind of listener that you are. Choose someone who will give you honest feedback.

1. Checking Up on Yourself

Fill out the following chart by circling the appropriate response to each statement.

1.	My actions indicate that I consider listening an important way to express love to another person.	Never Sometimes Usually
2.	Others would say that I am "slow to speak, and quick to hear."	Never Sometimes Usually
3.	I decide what I should listen for when someone talks to me.	Never Sometimes Usually
4.	I like to listen to people talk.	Never Sometimes Usually

5. I listen well to

children	Never	Sometimes	Usually
youth	Never	Sometimes	Usually
men	Never	Sometimes	Usually
women	Never	Sometimes	Usually
friends	Never	Sometimes	Usually
strangers	Never	Sometimes	Usually

2. Weekly Journaling

Begin a listening journal. After reading this chapter, finish each of the following statements in your journal:

- My listening would be more effective if I . . .
- What I want to gain from this book is . . .
- Two people I would like to ask to hold me accountable as a listener are . . .

3. Going Further

Using a concordance, which you'll find in the back of most Bibles, make a study of verses that describe God as a listener. Try to find out what God listens for, whom God listens to, and the response of those to whom God listens.

CHAPTER TWO

[Why Can't I Hear You?]

•

Why, what a wasp-stung and impatient fool art thou . . .
tying thine ear to no tongue but thine own.

William Shakespeare, *Henry IV*, Act I, Scene 3

A wise man learns by listening; the simpleton can learn
only by seeing scorners punished.

Proverbs 21:11 TLB

Rich and Jill Bright have been married for ten years.
Both would say they are pleased with their marriage and
have a growing love for each other. Yet Jill is troubled

31

by their communication patterns. Neither seems to hear the other at times when listening is important. Jill feels a void when she tries to tell Rich something that's significant to her and all he says is "uh huh." So she decided to do something. Let's have Rich tell what happened.*

•

"I call my wife 'Mrs. Impulsive,' so I wasn't completely surprised when she told me one Saturday morning that she had registered us for a marriage seminar the following weekend. She informed me that the topic would be how to be a more effective listener.

"'A listening seminar! Who needs that?' I asked. 'I hear just fine.'

"But along with her impulsiveness there is firm determination, so you guessed it. We went.

"I liked the seminar leader, Max, right away. He was a warm, engaging speaker who combined humor with convincing research and insights from the Bible. His opening statement grabbed me right away. He said, 'Listening is an unnatural process. It goes against our nature to listen perceptively.' Max made a persuasive case, demonstrating how inefficient most people are when it comes to hearing what others say.

> Listening is an
> unnatural process.
> It goes against
> our nature to listen
> perceptively.

"Max stressed the difference between *hearing* and *listening*. 'Hearing is connected to the physical process by which we receive sounds in our brain,' he said. 'It's an

---

* What follows is an imaginary account of a seminar on listening. Rich and Jill Bright and the people mentioned in Rich's account are not actual people, but all of these individuals as well as the issues they discuss are representative of my twenty years of experience in counseling and leading seminars.

automatic process that occurs without noticeable effort. Listening, however, is *a skill one learns*. The skilled listener has developed the ability to separate facts, innuendos, distractions, emotions, just to name a few.' He went on to stress that we learn to perceive or to ignore voices, music, noises—the sounds that surround us. We learn to 'tune in' or 'tune out.'

"A muscular fellow named Jorge said that this reminded him of a 'Dennis the Menace' cartoon he had seen. Dennis goes to Mr. Wilson, his neighbor, who is reading the newspaper, and gives him a warm, 'Hello, Mr. Wilson.' But his neighbor makes no reply. So Dennis turns up the volume. 'Hello, Mr. Wilson!' Still no response. In desperation Dennis blasts forth with 'HELLO, MR. WILSON!' The man continues to ignore Dennis. Then as Dennis turns to leave he speaks in a normal voice saying, 'Well, then, goodbye, Mr. Wilson.' Mr. Wilson replies, 'Goodbye, Dennis.' As he walks out the door Dennis remarks, 'There's nothing wrong with his hearing, but his listening's not so good.'

"Everyone laughed, but inwardly I felt embarrassed. Just the day before, Danny, my nine-year-old, had wanted to tell me about his baseball game, but I had ignored him because I wanted to finish an article in *Sports Illustrated*. Max was hitting too close to home.

"After the laughter had subsided, Max reminded us that many things determine how motivated we are to listen. 'All kinds of things determine your capacity to be a perceptive listener.' Then he asked, 'When are you a poor listener?'

"It probably wasn't that long, but it seemed like there was silence for about a minute before Lisa spoke. 'When I'm defensive I don't seem to hear a thing. Yesterday, a coworker brought up a problem between us that we've not resolved. I could feel my mental and emotional barriers go up like a steel curtain. I may have looked calm on the outside, but internally I was making my list of all the reasons he was wrong and I was right. And the problem is not limited to the office.' She turned to her husband and said, 'I do the same thing to you.'

•

"When I'm defensive I don't seem to hear a thing."

•

"Lisa's confession triggered a lot of comments from our group. Max broke in saying, 'It's obvious that *defensiveness* is a common problem in the way we communicate. I call these interactions *duelogues* rather than *dialogues*.

"'We're busy thinking up an effective remark so we can shoot down the other person's comments. And because we're not listening perceptively, we distort or downright ignore some of the most important data and emotional aspects of what the other person is trying to express.'

"I thought of another thing that complicates this issue—defensiveness can remain underground within the listener. Outwardly she may give meek agreement or simply remain silent. But on the inside, she is carrying on a heated conversation, denying what the speaker is saying, justifying her actions, or shifting the blame to someone else. Her mental energy is being consumed in nonlistening activities.

"Max reminded us that we *learn* to be defensive. The good news is that we can learn a more helpful form of relating. We can become more sensitive to situations in which we habitually raise our defenses, and we can practice more profitable listening habits.

"I made a mental note to myself to give this business of defensiveness more thought.

"Our leader again asked the question, 'When are you a poor listener?' From the back of the room I heard a man with a strong, assertive voice say, 'I'm a talker. Maybe it's some ego need I have—I don't know. But I do know that I get more satisfaction from talking than from listening. If you make me be quiet too long, I can hardly contain myself. I want to jump in and give everybody my two cents worth!

"'Both my wife and I know how this shapes our relationship. She's told me a million times that I'm not sensitive to her needs. She starts to talk, I get impatient and butt in, and then she tells me she feels violated. Her response is to stop talking.'

•

"I'm a talker. Maybe it's some ego need I have— I don't know."

•

"Someone in the front of the room said, 'Why don't you memorize James 1:19—"be quick to listen, slow to speak!"' Everyone laughed.

"Max made one of his insightful comments. 'Often we don't listen to others because we are too caught up in listening to ourselves. We don't listen well to two competing messages.' I heard my conscience say to me, 'That's you, buddy!'

"'Too many of us,' continued Max, 'aren't sold on the rich reward of being a perceptive listener. We need to see what an expression of love it is to encourage others to speak and then involve ourselves in listening intently, becoming genuinely interested in what the other person is sharing.'

"I was reminded of an observation my friend Matthew had made recently about listening. When he said it, it hit me as really significant. He said, 'Every issue of sin has its root in selfishness. And listening is a selfless act because you are orienting yourself to the other person, not yourself. That's why so many of us are poor listeners.'

•

Often we don't listen to others because we are too caught up in listening to ourselves.

•

"'Before we move on,' said Max, 'let me remind you that interrupting, like defensiveness, is a habit we learn.

It may be stimulated by our ego-centeredness, or it may be due to impatience with others. Whatever the reason, *interrupting is a sure way to turn off the other person.* In dealing with this obstacle, we may need not only to work on breaking the habit but also work on letting God show us our self-centeredness and help us become more relaxed and patient.

> • Interrupting is a sure way to turn off the other person. •

"'When else are you a poor listener?' Max asked.

"Calvin's answer moved us into a third area of poor listening. He said, 'My wife, Marie, has helped me see that I often overload people with too much data.

"'I can ramble on for five minutes without taking a breath. My wife has reminded me many times that I'm like a dump truck trying to dump the whole load at once. The listener gets smothered. They can't digest all that information. My challenge is to speak in shorter bursts and let the other person absorb a reasonable amount of info.'

"Calvin's insights set me to thinking and two thoughts immediately surfaced in my own mind. One, Calvin was identifying a *speaker* problem that hinders effective listening. The first two had been primarily listener problems. I can see that the speaker, too, can create situations or obstacles that hinder perceptive listening.

"The other thought related to an incident that happened at work a few days before. I was in my office when a fellow worker came to my door and asked to speak with me. He was enthusiastic about a new idea he had. He began to speak and went on for fifteen minutes. During that time, I needed to ask questions, but he gave me no opportunity. When he was finally finished, I felt weary from having listened for such a long period to so much information.

"A woman sitting beside Lisa entered the discussion. She said, 'I've had the problem we're discussing, but I am learning to speak for shorter periods of time. It hasn't been easy, but I find that by breaking five minutes of monologue into one-minute units, I give my listener an opportunity to digest what I've said. If something needs clarifying, he can ask a question. If he wants to express his opinion or give additional information, he can. What I like best about this is that it helps keep my listener involved. He not only listens but responds.'

"Max moved us on with the same question he'd been probing us with. This time a woman with a soft voice spoke (I had to really listen to hear all that she said). 'I don't listen well when I have other things pressing in on me,' she said. 'My mind flits back and forth and I become confused. What can I do about it?'

"Immediately a slender lady with a ponytail raised her hand, and her eyes lit up as she spoke. 'I can identify with that. Yesterday a friend phoned to share a difficult problem she was experiencing. I had just put something in the microwave, and I needed to watch the time. In comes Marty, our seven-year-old, to tell me about the problem he's having with his sister. I felt like I was playing ping pong, tossing horseshoes, and skiing all at the same time! Finally, out of desperation, I told my friend that I'd call her back after supper so we could talk further.'

•

I don't listen well when I have other pressing things on my mind.

•

"A lot of us nodded our heads, identifying with this problem. Max addressed the issue saying, 'Actually, two separate problems may be involved here.' He spoke first of *internal* distractions or concerns which hinder effective listening. 'Though nothing in the room distracts me, things in my mind do: I'm worried about whether my son got back to college safely; I keep thinking about a disturbing remark my wife made as I left for work; I'm bothered that I'm not prepared for the test I have tomorrow. It's difficult to listen because I'm conscious of all the work I must accomplish today.'

"Max gave us some help. 'You can say, "I'd like to continue listening, but I'm so pressured with a work deadline that I can't concentrate well on our conversation. Could we talk further this evening?" Or, you can discipline your mind to lay aside the competing problem and focus on an immediate concern.'

"Max spoke about one fact that I'd never heard before, but it made sense to me. He pointed out that a listener could think at between four hundred to seven hundred words per minute. But a speaker speaks at a rate of one hundred twenty-five to two hundred words per minute. So what does the mind do with this extra thinking time? You got it. We take little mental side trips to explore our fantasies, to think through recent events, to ponder personal problems, to entertain ourselves.

"Max told us that the individual committed to perceptive listening must learn to concentrate on what the speaker is saying. He has to take charge of his thought process and develop a way to actively work with what the speaker is saying and feeling. He uses his energy to reinforce his listening, not to ignore the speaker.

"Then Max addressed a second problem, saying that it relates to *external* distractions or competing speakers. He said, 'Imagine that your favorite team is in the championship play-offs; it's the final game, and it's being televised. In fact, you're watching it right now. The doorbell rings. In come your brother and sister-in-law, who are passing through town and only have three hours to visit with you. You turn the TV down so you can talk *and* watch—right? Now you're trying to listen to both the game and your brother. It will likely be frustrating for both of you. Yet you're unwilling to give up either one.'

"As we discussed this listening problem, we agreed that those who need to be heard can help the listener by choosing the appropriate time to discuss personal matters—not when the listener is distracted by someone or something else. Sometimes we accuse others of being poor listeners when we have approached them at unsuitable times.

"'Our time is almost over,' Max said, 'but could someone give me one more example of when you are a poor listener?'

"We got our response from Arnie. 'Shawna, my wife, and I have been frustrated with our communication patterns. We try to discuss important issues at the wrong time. When I am bone tired, I just don't have the energy to listen well.

"'Bedtime is definitely out. I end up fighting to stay awake, and Shawna becomes frustrated or angry. Then I feel guilty because I can't listen to what she wants to share. We wised up and resolved this by setting aside time to talk when we're rested and alert.'

"In the discussion that followed, we came to see that as well as physical fatigue, our emotional and mental weariness dulled our 'listenability.' Many of our twentieth-century vocations tax mental and emotional energy as much or more than physical energy. When husband and/or wife comes home from work, they may want to escape serious conversations.

"I recalled numerous incidents when I had returned home from exhausting mental work to be greeted by a lovely wife and three excited children who wanted to update me on their day's activities. I had learned to be honest with them, telling them when I needed fifteen minutes to relax before relating.

"As I pondered all that had been said, I discovered one more listening obstacle that I'd struggled with. Turning to my group members, I said, 'I confess to another listening barrier! In reflecting on our discussion, I see that I have biases that keep me from being a perceptive listener. This discussion has helped me to see where I need to grow.

"'I've erected listening barriers *toward certain individuals*. I can think of a person I work with whom I regularly turn off. Just the tone of her voice sends me into orbit. She has that whiny pitch that can give a person a migraine headache in about ten minutes. I pity her husband. Also, her constant complaining irritates me. I find her a very difficult person to listen to.'

> •
>
> I confess! I've erected listening barriers toward certain individuals.
>
> •

"The other group members nodded their heads, and I knew they could identify with what I was describing. It's a problem that can infect both men and women. I recalled Jill telling me of a conversation she had with her girlfriend Paula. Paula is really down on men and is convinced that all men are jerks. Her attitude is that they don't have anything worthwhile to say so why listen to them.

"We can hold biased attitudes toward the opposite sex, different age groups (teens are weird; they don't know much), ethnic minorities, certain personality types, and so on. Failing to listen seriously to members of these groups is one specific way we express these attitudes.

"After summarizing what we had discovered, Max dismissed us for the evening. As my wife and I walked back to our room, I summarized again in my mind the obstacles we had explored. I decided that I needed to develop an approach to coping with obstacles to listening. I wanted to be a perceptive listener. Thus in the days that followed I worked to develop a practical plan of action."

•

Rich's experience at the seminar helped him get in touch with a number of obstacles to effective listening. As we profit from his insights, it would be helpful to summarize some of the listening barriers that were discussed. I am less likely to be a perceptive listener when

- I am defensive
- I have an ego-centered need to talk
- I receive more information than I can digest
- I am confronted with internal or external distractions
- I am physically, emotionally, or mentally fatigued
- I have erected barriers toward individuals

Fortunately, we don't have to be defeated by these barriers. Help is available. Let's move on to explore our options.

Five Ways to Remove Listening Obstacles

Identify the obstacle. What is the specific obstacle or obstacles that hinder your ability to listen—your *listenability*? Of the seven mentioned in this chapter, which limits you most? This will be the one on which you want to focus your energy first.

It is also helpful to identify the person or persons who are most affected by the obstacle. Does your defensiveness hinder your communication most when you are talking with your spouse? Your children? Your boss? By identifying the person, you become more aware of the relationship that needs the most attention.

Identify who controls the obstacle. If you are defensive, then you control the obstacle because it is within you (though another's comments may encourage or discourage defensiveness). The one with the "urge to talk" controls the obstacle more than the listener does. Poor timing is more likely to be a problem controlled both by the listener and the one who wants to talk.

Identifying who controls the obstacle is important because it helps you see whether the problem is yours or another person's. Once this is identified, you may have to work with the people involved to *rearrange the conditions* in order to develop a more satisfying communication process. Rearranging the conditions may involve working on defensiveness, finding a better place to talk, applying a specific communication principle, and so on.

Determine the level of commitment. Do you want to change your present behavior or attitudes? How important is it to you to change patterns that defeat good communication? What will it cost? Are you ready to expend the energy necessary to work for personal growth daily? Are you committed to listen, even when the speaker is not motivating? (I'm told that a polite person is one who listens intently to things he already knows about, from an individual who knows nothing about them!)

Develop sensitivity to defeating situations. When are you usually physically fatigued? Toward whom do you hold unhealthy attitudes? What internal pressures typically erode your ability to listen?

This step acquaints us with the facts and circumstances related to our listening obstacles. If a wife comes to see that Thursday night is typically a difficult time because her husband wants to talk, but she is always worn out, then she will want to focus her energy on changing the Thursday night defeat pattern.

Work out a practical plan. What would be one practical step to change the situation? In the illustration above it might be to (1) take an afternoon nap, (2) schedule supper later so she can talk when her husband gets home, (3) go out for supper to a quiet, relaxing environment, or (4) agree to talk after supper and after both have had an hour to relax.

Usually, there is some practical step you can take to begin to move from obstacle to opportunity. Will you commit yourself to work on the solution? In the "Time to Reflect and Apply" section to follow, you will find some practical ways to work at removing any of the obstacles that hinder your ability to listen.

Time to Reflect and Apply

Rich's story contains a lot of helpful information about how listening obstacles can hinder effective communication—and how they can be overcome. The following exercises are designed to help you remove your own listening obstacles. In working through the exercises, try to be as practical as possible. Work out solutions and determine which obstacle is most important to tackle *this* week.

1. Checking Up on Yourself

Circle the appropriate response to each statement. This will help you apply what you have learned.

1. I listen even when I don't like the person who is talking.   Never   Sometimes   Usually

2. I cope positively with
   external distractions   Never   Sometimes   Usually
   internal distractions   Never   Sometimes   Usually

3. I dominate conversations.	Never	Sometimes	Usually
4. I am a defensive listener.	Never	Sometimes	Usually
5. I use poor timing when I want to talk.	Never	Sometimes	Usually
6. I'm prone to dumping too much data on people.	Never	Sometimes	Usually
7. I can put what I'm doing out of my mind when someone wants to talk to me.	Never	Sometimes	Usually
8. I can identify situations in which I am a poor listener. I know how to cope with them.	Never	Sometimes	Usually
9. I interrupt others when they are speaking.	Never	Sometimes	Usually
10. I am prone to daydreaming when I listen to someone for a long time.	Never	Sometimes	Usually
11. I get impatient with a speaker and finish what he is saying.	Never	Sometimes	Usually

It's always a great idea to get feedback. Why not ask someone to indicate how he or she would rate you in these eleven areas?

2. Weekly Journaling

Summarize what you have learned from this chapter that will be the most helpful. What obstacles keep you from being a more perceptive listener? Jot down examples of when they have occurred this past week. What specific steps can you take to help you overcome the obstacle? Think through the following bad listening habits. Which ones do you think you have learned? Choose one to concentrate on changing.

- Ignoring others when reading the newspaper or watching television
- Asking a family member to listen when he or she is weary, busy, or upset
- Talking for too long without allowing the listener to respond
- Interrupting others while they are talking
- Becoming defensive when someone tells you about a problem or weakness he or she sees in you
- Falling asleep in church or Sunday school

3. Going Further

Fill in the chart as completely as possible. Base your answers on your own experiences. Identify which is the biggest problem for you.

Obstacles to Effective Listening	Toward Whom	Recent Example	Practical Steps toward Solution
Defensiveness			
Urge to talk			
Information overload			
Internal/external pressures			
Poor timing			
Physical/mental fatigue			
Negative attitude			

CHAPTER THREE

[Listening with Your Eyes]

•

By a man's finger-nails, by his coat-sleeve, by his boots, by his trouser-knees, by the calluses of his forefinger and thumb, by his expression, by his shirt-cuff—by each of these things a man's calling is plainly revealed. That all united should fail to enlighten the competent inquirer in any case is almost inconceivable.[1]

Sherlock Holmes

A scoundrel and villain who goes about with a corrupt mouth, who winks with his eye, signals with his feet and motions with his fingers, who plots evil with deceit in his heart—he always stirs up dissension.

Proverbs 6:12–14

Mark entered my office. He scanned the room as though he were looking for an adversary. Then he walked to the sofa and collapsed. He drummed his fingers on the arm. He squirmed, trying to get comfortable. When he crossed his legs, his left foot bounced nervously. Finally our eyes met and I could see the fear. He took a deep breath and blurted out, "I'm in trouble."

From the moment Mark opened the door, he was communicating. Though he didn't speak, his every move gave me some indication of what was going on internally.

This incident shows the importance nonverbal communication plays in perceptive listening. Looking for nonverbal cues that support—or conflict—with a spoken message is an integral part of effective listening. One writer reminds us that a person cannot avoid communicating. Though she may decide to stop talking, it is impossible for her to stop behaving. The behavior of a person—her facial expression, posture, gestures, and other actions—provide an uninterrupted stream of information and a constant source of clues to the feelings she is experiencing. The reading of body language, therefore, is one of the most significant skills of good listening.[2]

Importance of Nonverbal Communication

The study of nonverbal communication in human relationships is extensive. In fact, it can become quite technical and complex. However, my purpose is not to investigate it from this perspective. My concern is with the practical implications of nonverbal behavior for the perceptive listener.

First, let me define what I mean by nonverbal communication.

Nonverbal communication includes every means of communication you consciously or unconsciously employ. This includes the *way* you speak, the vocal cues that support your message, and the emphasis you place on certain words. It also embraces all your body cues and emotional expressions. Even the way you dress communicates a message. For example, I like to wear shirts that are bright and colorful to show my zest for life.

Most of us pick up on nonverbal cues whether we are conscious of it or not. Sometimes we feel an emotion that tells us we are "reading" another's nonverbal communication. Or we watch another person and know they are mad or that they had a hard day.

Few people fully grasp the importance of nonverbal communication, despite the fact that it is common knowledge among communication researchers that approximately 60 to 65 percent of our meaning is expressed nonverbally.[3] Communication can be divided into three components, as illustrated in the diagram below.

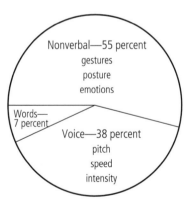

My encounter with Mark demonstrates this threefold aspect. I gathered a significant amount of data about this young man *before he spoke.* I could have anticipated that something was troubling him, even if he had never said a word. But even when he did speak, I was "reading" his tone of voice, his verbal speed, and his intensity.

Nonverbal cues are not only important to the listener, but also the speaker profits from knowing about nonverbal communication as well. The speaker then can decipher the listener's response by listening with her eyes. She sees the listener's reaction to her message. If I intend to be an effective communicator, I must develop my skill at reading nonverbal communication. As I counsel, teach, and preach, I am conscious of how my audience is responding to what I am saying. If I use humor in my presentation and no one laughs, I must evaluate what I'm doing and make some midcourse corrections.

Which brings us to a fascinating point: some individuals become effective at removing obvious nonverbal cues. They hide actions or feelings that would give away inner emotions. When this happens, the listener is left with fewer clues to understand what the speaker is feeling or thinking. He or she has to work from the spoken message alone. When my son Joel jokes with my wife, my wife usually finds it difficult to tell that it is in humor because he is skillful at masking his nonverbal cues.

> If I intend to be an effective communicator, I must develop my skill at reading nonverbal communications.

An understanding of nonverbal communication is a valuable aid to adult-child relationships. Children are limited in their ability to understand the meanings of words. They are more skilled at reading our tone of voice, our physical touches, and our facial expressions. It is fascinating to observe that Jesus laid his hands on the children to express his love and blessing on them (Matt. 19:15).

How Nonverbal Cues Communicate

The more we examine this topic, the more we see the many ways we communicate without words. However, before we go on, a word of caution may be helpful. I have already used the word "cues" to speak of nonverbal communication. This word suggests a hint or intimation, the presence of an underlying attitude or meaning. We must guard against judging a person's attitude, motive, or meaning based entirely on nonverbal expressions. Rather, we should treat these as clues that can lead us to further insight, or as indicators that we need to seek additional information from the speaker.

Body Cues

There are three kinds of nonverbal communication. The first are *body cues*. Body cues include all the ways our bodies support, confuse, or deny a spoken message. If we are alert, we pick up the message.

BODY POSITION

Our body position gives cues to the listener. If we are weary or discouraged, we might slouch in a chair; if we are anxious, we might sit tensely or move nervously. Sometimes the way we position ourselves in relation to other people communicates our underlying attitudes or concerns. If we become frustrated with a group decision, we may express our withdrawal by sliding our chair back slightly and sitting quietly outside the circle. We express fear, confrontation, or affection by our degree of physical proximity (e.g., backing away, "nose to nose," arm around shoulder).

One of my most humiliating experiences in college related to my body language. For an assignment in Miss Taylor's storytelling class, I had to tell a story in front of my classmates. I felt nervous and foolish standing before the class. Just as I got under way, Miss Taylor stopped me, came to the front, and began to tell me about my poor body posture. My face was red just trying to tell the story, but when my professor decided to straighten me out, I went beet red. As you can see, I've never forgotten the experience.

I have a book in my library that illustrates 132 distinct body postures that a person can assume. None include facial expressions. When I looked through the different postures, I was surprised at the potential messages that could be communicated through the majority of the body positions—even unknowingly. That's something we need to recognize; we may be sending a message without realizing it.

Facial Expressions

Another form of body language is communicated through our *facial expressions*. Our faces can show that we feel happy, solemn, despondent, or excited, to name a few. If the corners of our mouth turn up, we generally communicate happiness; if they turn down, the message we give is one of sadness or anger. The phrases "laughing eyes," "chin up," and "starry-eyed" all refer to facial forms of communication.

It is possible to identify at least sixteen different positions that the mouth alone may take. For example, you can smile slightly with the corners of your mouth; smile with a full smile—mouth closed; smile with your mouth open, exposing partial teeth; smile with your mouth fully open, exposing teeth and gums. Each position may communicate a distinct message.

GESTURES AND NERVOUS HABITS

Body cues also include *gestures and nervous habits*. Courses in public speaking attempt to teach us how to utilize effective hand motions to complement, support, and stress key points of our message. The uplifted hand communicates worship; the clenched fist, anger or warfare; the open, extended hand, welcome or greeting. Nervous habits include constant hand movement, hair pulling, twitching, nervous eye movements, and general restlessness.

THE WAY WE DRESS

A final body cue is the way we *dress*. We might ask, "Do clothes communicate?" Yes, our clothes say something about us without us saying a word. We may choose loud clothes to attract attention or dress sloppily as a reflection of a disorderly life or a spirit of rebellion. I work out at a local gym. Some individuals dress in casual T-shirts and shorts when they exercise. Other people come with tight fitting clothes that accent and reveal their bodies. They seem to want others to notice their sexuality. Think of people you know who always wear a ball cap or a shirt that carries a team logo. They want others to know that they are a Raiders' fan or follow the Arizona Diamondbacks. There is a definite relationship between clothes and communication. Consider the different functions that clothing serves listed below and how what people wear communicates that function.

1. Protection   5. Status
2. Sexuality   6. Assertiveness/denial
3. Group affiliation 7. Role
4. Concealment   8. Enhancement

Voice Cues

A second basic form of nonverbal communication is *voice cues*. As we speak, we embellish the message by volume, tone, and rate of speech. Voice cues greatly influence how people interpret and respond to a message. This is the wisdom of Proverbs 15:1, which reminds us that "A gentle answer turns away wrath, but a harsh word stirs up anger." The simple sentence "I love you" can range from positive to negative, depending on the tone and word emphasis. Proverbs also wisely notes, "If a man loudly blesses his neighbor early in the morning, it will be taken as a curse" (27:14).

Most of us use voice cues subconsciously as a way to express meanings, attitudes, or emotions of which we may be unaware. One person I know consistently uses a "yes, but" pattern of speech. When another person makes a comment or expresses an opinion, this person will frequently respond with "Yes, but" and proceed to show why the other person's idea is wrong. I confess that my early experiences with this person left me feeling put down by whatever I said because I felt it was a criticism of my ideas and me.

Emotional Cues

A third important form of nonverbal communication is *emotional cues*. Emotional expressions such as laughter, weeping, or giggling reveal inner states and heavily influence how our spoken message is interpreted. Emotional cues cause others to see us as warm or cool, friendly or hostile. Of course, some individuals are skilled at hiding their emotions, so we don't know what is taking place internally.

Characteristics of Nonverbal Communication

Nonverbal communication reveals itself in many forms, but certain characteristics are common to all kinds. Understanding these characteristics can help us both as speakers and as listeners. First, we use nonverbal communication to express or highlight our emotions. Feelings are ventilated more easily through nonverbal channels. One possible reason for this is that the emotions can work through the nonverbal routes subconsciously, whereas the verbal expression is dominated by the conscious mind. What we are reluctant or fearful to admit consciously, we will often release subconsciously. This seems safer although it is potentially more dangerous. Recently, a person was telling me about a phone conversation with a close friend. The caller was giving information in an informative way, but the tone of voice was harsh, abrupt, and demanding. My friend was upset because the nonverbal message felt more accurate than the verbal content. It made her question the caller's level of commitment to her.

> •
> Feelings
> are ventilated
> more easily through
> nonverbal channels.
> •

A second characteristic of nonverbal communication is that it is more ambiguous than spoken words. This makes it easier to confuse the message received. The listener must be very cautious and tentative in interpreting nonverbal communication. He should feed back his perceptions and seek confirmation from the speaker rather than assume he knows what the nonverbal expression means.

I want to underscore this point—*nonverbal communication is more difficult to interpret.* The individual who assumes he knows what the nonverbal information means may find himself mistaken. We can be skilled at carefully analyzing the data we are receiving, but we never can be positive of what is going on inside the other individual.

- Nonverbal communication is more difficult to interpret. -

My wife gives me an illustration of this point. There were times when she would give a big sigh with no words. The children and I were left to try and figure out what was going on. One day we talked about it so that we could understand just what was happening. She explained that at different times the sigh meant different things! We expressed our confusion, and she realized that she needed to let us know more accurately what she was feeling.

The following chart helps you see how easily we can be confused or deceived by what we are observing. The wise listener will be committed to checking out his observations to clarify his accuracy. Only then can he be certain that he is on target.

Visible Action or Appearance	Could Mean	Or It Could Mean
Crying	Happiness	Unhappiness
Silence	Withdrawal and disinterest	Active involvement through careful thought
Laughter	"I'm laughing at you."	"I'm laughing with you."
Tearing up	Despair	Deep gratitude to God

Feeding back what we observe to the speaker and seeking more information is the most reliable way to clarify nonverbal data.

Another characteristic of nonverbal communication is its limited scope. While the nonverbal can be more powerful, more intense, than the spoken message, it does not have the range of communication. It is much more limited in expressing concepts and ideas. *It is best to think of nonverbal communication as a different form of communication with different potential and different limitations.* Then we learn to draw from it what it can give, but not expect it to give the full message. We let the verbal and nonverbal complement each other.

> •
> Nonverbal communication's primary function is to reinforce or undergird the verbal.
> •

I must emphasize that nonverbal communication is not less important than verbal. Its primary function is to reinforce or undergird the verbal. It fills speech with greater vitality. Without it, verbal communication would become dull and lifeless.

Four Keys to Listening for the Nonverbal

Skill in listening for nonverbal communication is vital to becoming an effective listener. Often it is the physical signals that help us most in pursuing the underlying meaning of a spoken message. The following four guidelines will help you become more adept at picking up these cues.

Become sensitized to nonverbal cues. Discipline yourself to look for body language, voice cues, and emotional expressions. At first you may have to plan to observe these signs, but eventually alertness to nonverbal signals will become a way of life.

As sensitivity to nonverbal cues increases, it is wise to learn to check out your perceptions with the speaker. It is always a good idea to *document what you observe* rather than merely giving an opinion. Documenting means that you tell the person what you have observed: "For the past five minutes you've been wringing your hands." Try not to interpret what you've seen, but if you do, make it clear that the interpretation is based on what you observed. "For the past five minutes you've been wringing your hands; are you anxious about the decision you've made?"

Realize that verbal and nonverbal messages should complement each other. In the book *Interpersonal Growth through Communication,* the authors suggest that we "must become much more aware of the messages we send. Remember that you may be sending more messages unintentionally than you are sending on purpose. Take time to ensure that your nonverbal messages are consistent with your intention and to ask for and to understand feedback from others."[4] This is an important clue for us as listeners as well as speakers. Do you sense any contradiction between what you are hearing verbally and what is coming across nonverbally? What is the nature of the contradiction?

When verbal and nonverbal do not harmonize, you have what is known as a *mixed message.* Mixed messages put an additional burden on listeners; they tell us something is not functioning properly. In such a case, you must feed back the mixed message to the speaker for clarification. For example, Rita comes into the room, slams the door, and crashes on the sofa. Her appearance is gloomy. Her friend Charles asks, "Are you unhappy about something?" Rita replies, "No."

Rita is sending a mixed message; her behavior is not consistent with her spoken communication. So Charles says, "Rita, you said you're not unhappy, but you slammed the door and plopped on the sofa, and you look very dejected." Notice that Charles documented what he saw. As he shares his observation with her, Rita is able to see the discrepancy between her verbal and nonverbal messages.

In listening, it is helpful to think of the various sources of input that we're receiving from different channels, then look for congruence among the various channels, especially between verbal and nonverbal. We can then ask ourselves, "Is the message I'm receiving consistent?" If not, we can clarify the issue by sharing what we observe with the speaker.

Recognize that a listener is more apt to believe the nonverbal than the verbal message. This is important information for you as a speaker. Nonverbal cues can color a listener's perception of what the speaker is saying. It is harder to cover up the nonverbal. The person who does not want to admit that he is upset cannot avoid being restless, fidgeting with his hands, or showing other nervous behavior.

•

Recognize that
a listener is more
apt to believe
the nonverbal than
the verbal message.

•

At the time I am writing this, Representative Gary Condit, from the state of California, is in the public eye because of a possible affair with one of his aides who has disappeared. When television reporter Connie Chung interviewed him, people polled following his interview expressed skepticism about his truthfulness. Much of the discussion surrounded questions he avoided answering. Even his own Democratic colleagues expressed lack of confidence in his answers.

When nonverbal behavior is too intense, it can block out or distort verbal communication. The person in distress cannot think clearly and thus is unable to speak clearly. The person struggling with anger speaks from that anger and it colors the spoken message.

Realize that the same cue can express a variety of feelings. For this reason, remember to check out nonverbal cues. Family members and work associates frequently "read into" another's actions those ideas, motives, and

59

feelings they believe that person has. This can lead to judgmental attitudes that are destructive to close relationships. One of the root causes of communication breakdown is our tendency to judge an individual's intentions from nonverbal cues that we observe. In fact, it is not uncommon to find damaged relationships stemming from misperception of nonverbal cues.

> •
> One of the root causes of communication breakdown is our tendency to judge an individual's intentions from nonverbal cues that we observe.
> •

The wise listener determines to withhold judgment on nonverbal cues, choosing rather to feed back his or her observations in a nonthreatening, nonjudgmental form. The speaker can then confirm or clarify those observations. A communication process built on this foundation has high potential to lead to positive relationships.

During one of my writing breaks, I was sharing with Winnie my opening illustration of Mark. She laughed and said, "You should tell about my nonverbal behavior this morning. You heard pots and pans banging loudly, matched by my voice, so you came out into the kitchen and said, 'Winnie, is something wrong?' You received my nonverbal message!" We laughed together and I thanked her for such a relevant illustration for ending this chapter! I've learned that when Winnie slams cupboard doors, I need to tune in and listen. A message is being sent!

Time to Reflect and Apply

To help you apply the concepts described in this chapter, I suggest that you work through the following exercises. They will increase your sensitivity to nonverbal behavior.

1. Checking Up on Yourself

The following statements will help you do a bit of self-evaluation of your nonverbal communication skills.

1. I use appropriate nonverbal actions to encourage others to speak—smile, nod my head, etc.	Never	Sometimes	Usually
2. I recognize the presence of nonverbal cues when I am listening to another person.	Never	Sometimes	Usually
3. Because nonverbal communication is difficult to interpret, I do not make decisions about what it means without first checking it out with the speaker.	Never	Sometimes	Usually
4. I seek clarification when I am getting a mixed message.	Never	Sometimes	Usually
5. I realize that the same nonverbal cue can express a range of feelings, so I avoid being dogmatic about their meaning.	Never	Sometimes	Usually
6. I understand that I am more apt to believe nonverbal cues than the verbal message, so I guard against that tendency.	Never	Sometimes	Usually

2. Weekly Journaling

During this week keep an account of the nonverbal communication that you observe in your family and friends.

3. Going Further

1. Turn on your television set but leave the volume off. Choose a program that portrays people communicating in life situations. In your notebook, jot down the nonverbal behaviors you observe and what messages they might be communicating. If possible, do this viewing with another person. Then compare your perceptions.
2. Discuss what nonverbal behaviors a person might display if he or she is feeling:

a. nervous	g. happy
b. fearful	h. angry
c. lonely	i. shy
d. rejected	j. loved
e. insecure	k. inferior
f. bored	l. secure

CHAPTER FOUR

[Listening with Your Heart]

•

Listening is a magnetic and strange thing, a creative force. The friends who listen to us are the ones we move toward, and we want to sit in their radius. When we are listened to, it creates us, makes us unfold and expand.[1]

Karl Menninger

A joyful heart makes a cheerful face, but when the heart is sad, the spirit is broken.

Proverbs 15:13 NASB

Meg has been a volunteer at a crisis hotline center for five years and has learned how to hear with both her ears and her heart. She listens intently as Teri pours out her story.

Teri has called before so Meg knows something of her background. She is involved in student government at Blair High School, is a straight A student, and volunteers at Lincoln Hospital. You'd think that she had the world in the palm of her hand. The truth is she feels a deep loneliness that has been there for a long time. Her family and friends see her as cheerful and full of fun, but that is a mask hiding an inner emptiness that never goes away.

Both parents hold demanding, full-time jobs, so they come home physically, mentally, and emotionally drained. For the past three years, stress in the home has been building. The marriage was the first place the breakdown began to be felt. Then, like cancer, it crept into other family members' lives. Teri's early memories of laughter and play at home are all that is left of the good times.

She describes to Meg the pain and sadness she feels over her deteriorating home life.

"It hurts to see my parents verbally attacking each other all the time," she laments. "The constant hostility is unbearable; I want to run away to some peaceful place. We all seem to spend more time in separate rooms. It's obvious that Mom and Dad are heading for a divorce, and I'm certain that it will be messy when it goes to court. Both are pigheaded, so neither is going to give an inch.

"Added to this, Mom has been expressing more anger toward me. The closeness we used to have is nearly gone. Meg, I hate being caught between her and Dad, but unless I side with her on every issue, she accuses me of betraying her. It's a no-win situation for me. I see the good and bad in both of my parents. I really want a relationship with them, but each wants me on his or her side, and if I don't side with that person, he or she is mean and hateful to me.

"Last Wednesday Mom blew up when I said that she is as responsible for the marriage as Dad is. She swore at me and called me—never mind—I won't say what she said. But it hurt awfully. I went to my room and cried for half an hour. Then I felt down for the rest of the day.

"Sometimes I think about running away to have some peace and quiet, but so far I haven't done it. I really don't want to, but it's getting harder and harder to cope. I can see why some of my friends are messing around with drugs.

"I think the worst part is that they don't listen to me. Oh, I guess they hear the words sometimes, but they don't really hear me. What can I do?"

Meg realizes that advice may not be what Teri needs right now. What she's really asking for is the love, compassion, and support of a caring person. Teri's goal is to communicate as much of that as she can by being an understanding friend and perceptive listener.

Helping Others through Perceptive Listening

Perceptive listening is a powerful tool for helping others. This has been consistently confirmed in over four decades of my adult life. The incentive to write this book came from countless situations in which individuals expressed gratitude because I listened.

One of the most important places I've practiced perceptive listening has been with my own family members. Over twenty-five years ago our family moved from southern California to Arizona. During a house-hunting trip to Phoenix, Amy, our oldest daugh-

•

Perceptive listening is a powerful tool for helping others.

•

ter, vented heated criticism about the move. I recall one statement: "Why would anyone want to live in that stupid cow-patch town!" Winnie and I were baffled because Amy is typically a cheerful, positive person.

Eventually the real problem surfaced during a conversation between Amy and her mother. As Winnie listened our daughter poured out her anxiety, and it helped Winnie see what we had overlooked. Amy was frightened at the prospect of leaving her friends behind, moving to a strange city, and entering a new school. As my wife and I more fully identified with her feelings, we were able to be supportive and understanding. Perceptive listening was the key.

Once we looked at the situation through her eyes and felt her emotions, her words and actions made sense. I felt a sense of relief because I knew what the root of my daughter's anxiety was. I knew how to pray for her and to support her in the transition. It helped Amy because she knew that her mother and I cared about her feelings and would be there to listen.

> •
> Our conversations are filled with emotions, some obvious to the eye and ear and others leaking their way out more subtly.
> •

You too can learn this powerful method of touching others' lives. It begins by listening for the feelings behind the words.

Our conversations are filled with emotions, some obvious to the eye and ear and others leaking their way out more subtly. It's our job as perceptive listeners to listen for these emotions and even to help draw them out.

There are three reasons this helps. First, it is a *powerful method for showing empathy* for what someone else is experiencing. We are consistently touching the lives of people who are lonely, depressed, disappointed, shy, unloved, fearful, and frustrated. When we empathize with them, we try to identify with their feelings, conflicts, and emotions; we try to relate to them in a genuine, caring manner. We may not necessarily agree with their behavior or lifestyle, but we "weep with those who weep" (Rom. 12:15). In order to empathize with others, however, we must determine just what they are feeling—and this requires perceptive listening.

Second, as we listen for feelings, we frequently *help others get in touch with their own emotions.* We act like a mirror, reflecting a person's feelings back to him in such a way that he is able to understand more clearly what he is feeling. It is not uncommon for someone to share his conflicts with a good listener and in the process discover feelings he was not even aware of—feelings that were stewing beneath the surface.

•

Emotions can build up like air being forced into a balloon.

•

Third, it *helps the speaker ventilate emotions* that are causing problems. Emotions can build up like air being forced into a balloon. The pressure gets higher and higher until it seems as though the balloon will burst. Talking out feelings of anger with a compassionate listener, for instance, often helps reduce the intensity of it and frees the speaker to work on constructive solutions. When I express my anxiety or fear to someone who doesn't laugh at me, or preach a sermon, or glibly state that "Christians shouldn't fear," it can enable me to process those emotions in a beneficial manner.

•

The perceptive listener provides a safe and healthy way to deflate and restore balance and wholeness to life.

•

The perceptive listener provides a safe and healthy way to deflate and restore balance and wholeness to life.

Of course, talking out feelings is not a guarantee that they will be resolved, but it is an early part of the problem-solving process that can lead to positive results. Perceptive listening is an essential part of that process.

How Does Perceptive Listening Help?

You and I can be of invaluable help to others as they endeavor to identify and process their emotions. Everyone we talk to will closely monitor us to see if it is safe to speak honestly and express inner emotions openly. They will look to see if we really care or if we are merely trying to be polite and act as though we are listening. Most people are very discerning and can tell the difference.

So what do we do? I have found the following three actions are helpful: *encourage the speaker to express his feelings.* I focus on getting the speaker to elaborate on his or her feelings. Then I listen without interrupting, or in any other way hindering the expression of feelings. One reason negative responses are not helpful is that by their nature they discourage the flow of feelings. They do not promote openness and release. They tend to imply, "Don't feel that way," "Don't say that," or "You're bad to have those feelings."

My own approach is to ask questions such as:

"How did you feel when she said _____ ?"
"Tell me what it felt like when _____ ."
"You said that you're feeling _____ . Tell me about it."

Try to put the other person in touch with her emotions. Frequently a person cannot clearly identify the emotion that is frustrating or defeating her. We can help her identify the underlying feelings by giving her freedom to speak about them and by sharing what we hear her saying. Sometimes perceptive questions ("Did you feel angry after he did that?") are helpful. Remember that one of the special strengths of perceptive listening is that it puts the speaker more in touch with her feelings.

Don't condemn feelings. Emotions are a part of human makeup. Sometimes they become difficult to control. Some emotions have been typed as "good" or "bad." Consequently, many people have developed a fear of expressing feelings.

Some people find it difficult to express *any* feelings. Others suppress certain feelings they perceive as unacceptable or inappropriate. The perceptive, caring listener attempts to give these individuals a secure environment in which to get in touch with these emotions and to talk them out.

Too often people create negative circumstances that inhibit true sharing. The troubled youth comes home from school only to be criticized because he's angry with his teacher. The wife wants someone with whom to share her feelings of insecurity, but her husband laughs about it. I share my discouragement in my small group at church, and I'm told, "Everyone feels like that at some time. You'll get over it in a day or two." Will we ever realize the potential ministry of the listening ear?

The Process of Listening for Emotions

Perceptive listening for emotions is a two-step process. Like any skill, once it is learned, it must be practiced until proficiency is gained.

69

Step 1: Listen for Feelings That Underlie Communication

Sounds simple, doesn't it? In practice it is much more difficult. Yet the point I have sought to make in this chapter is that this is a most helpful ministry and worth mastering. It pays rich dividends to the person in need. Last night I sat down with a young woman in our church family. During the conversation, she related the intense buildup of emotions that had been occurring during the preceding week. Misunderstandings in interpersonal relations were creating tensions that erratically flared up. For about forty-five minutes, I listened and helped my friend talk about the feelings being encountered.

At the conclusion of our discussion, the familiar smile had returned to my friend's face, and a renewed sense of confidence in God's power to undertake had emerged. My listening had allowed her to release pent-up emotions that were disabling her and robbing her of peace and joy. As she talked about her problem, the emotional tension subsided. She was able to think more clearly and solutions began to emerge.

Helping this young woman took more than just listening to her talk and nodding my head. I had to work at helping her understand what was going on inside of her. Perceptive listening for emotions is difficult for four reasons.

First, *emotions are not easily distinguished.* Is the person feeling moody or angry? Is it a feeling of superiority or inner confidence? Does she feel trapped or fearful to face old friends? We experience a broad range of emotions that we often are not even aware of.

Look at the following list. Which ones have you personally felt in recent days? How would you tell that someone else is feeling a particular feeling? What would you listen for? What would you look for?

Range of Emotions

Hurt	Inferior	Tense
Humiliated	Silly	Loved
Lonely	Jealous	Rejected
Intimidated	Sympathy	Disappointed
Hatred	Accepted	Frustrated
Hated	Protective	Impatient
Confident	Angry	Superior
Shy	Sad	Ashamed
Useless	Cheated	Trapped
Jubilant	Unworthy	Despair

You likely understand the dilemma that I'm describing. If you are a typical adult, you are not a feeling-sensitive person. Accurately identifying the feelings of others and clearly letting them know you care, is difficult work. Some people find it nearly impossible. Some give up without even trying.

When I first began to ponder this issue, I decided to develop a list of feelings that I could review. I soon found that other people wanted the list so that they could better identify their own feelings and the feelings they detected in others. One of the individuals that asked for a copy was my wife, Winnie. She posted the list on the inside of a cupboard door in our kitchen. When she knew that she was experiencing a feeling that she couldn't identify, she'd run to the cupboard, open the door, and scan the list. "Aha!" I'd hear her exclaim, "That's it! I'm feeling trapped."

Most of us have not practiced the skill of differentiating emotions enough to become proficient. Thus our capacity to understand ourselves and help others in this area is crippled.

The problem is even more complicated because we experience emotions on a continuum from mild to intense. The list that follows will help you see this movement from a less intense to a more intense expression of the same fundamental emotion.

Intensity of Emotions—Positive

Less Intense				More Intense
Aroused	Excited	Exhilarated	Thrilled	Ecstatic
Fond	Eager	Energetic	Avid	Passionate
Happy	Cheerful	Joyful	Overjoyed	Jubilant
Cuddled	Admired	Infatuated	Affection	Amorous
Awake	Perceptive	Aroused	Alert	Attentive
Recognized	Sought out	Appreciated	Valued	Prized
Calm	Mellow	Relaxed	Peaceful	Serene
Silly	Amused	Funny	Ridiculous	Hilarious
Surprised	Wonder	Intrigued	Astonished	Spellbound
Hopeful	Promising	Confident	Expectant	Optimistic
Liked	Applauded	Admired	Esteemed	Adored

Intensity of Emotions—Negative

Less Intense				More Intense
Thwarted	Disappointed	Disheartened	Heartbroken	Crushed
Misled	Manipulated	Deceived	Double-crossed	Betrayed
Blue	Sad	Sorrowful	Grieved	Overwhelmed
Nervous	Anxious	Afraid	Alarmed	Terrified
Irritated	Disgusted	Angry	Hostile	Vengeful
Sad	Apathetic	Despondent	Depressed	Suicidal
Deterred	Discouraged	Dejected	Distressed	Despair
Disgusted	Offended	Repelled	Repulsed	Horrified
Crabby	Sour	Sarcastic	Bitter	Hateful
Shy	Embarrassed	Ashamed	Stupid	Humiliated
Bored	Disinterested	Indifferent	Withdrawn	Isolated
Uncomfortable	Troubled	Hurt	Pain	Agony
Overlooked	Ignored	Rejected	Scorned	Banished
Uncertain	Doubtful	Skeptical	Unbelieving	Disdain
Erring	Wrong	Guilty	Evil	Wicked

The second factor that makes listening a challenge is that *many people are not in touch with their feelings and cannot articulate them clearly*. I grew up in a home where expressing or talking about our emotions was discouraged. Thus I was not comfortable with my feelings. As I grew older, I insulated myself from them, fearing the consequences if they were released. My dad was a harsh, no-nonsense person. When I'd cry, he threatened me with, "Stop that sniveling or I'll give you something to cry about." I knew he meant it, so I "turned off" the internal cry switch. When I became an adult, I recognized that appropriate crying was healthy, but I didn't know where the switch was.

One of the most important transformations that has occurred in my adulthood has been learning to identify and express my emotions in positive, healthy ways. My wife, Winnie, and loving friends have nurtured this and created a safe place where I could take new steps. The process I've gone through has helped me identify with others who are emotionally barren. Sam, a man in his early twenties who attended my church, is a good example.

One day Sam asked me if he could talk over a problem with me. He told me that over the past few years he had had three serious relationships with young women. After the first relationship came to an end, he had met another young woman whom he had developed strong feelings for. Sam said, "When Denise broke off with me, it hurt awfully. So when I met Paula, I determined not to get so emotionally involved. I didn't want to get hurt a second time. Yet as the relationship progressed, strong emotions began to surface. Then Paula ended the relationship just like Denise had. I again went through the emotional withdrawal."

Sam came to me because he was now in a relationship with Sheri and had carefully encapsulated his emotions to protect himself from further hurt. Sadly this relationship was ending because Sheri was seeking a relationship with a man who could be more emotionally expressive. Sam was trapped in a defensive pattern that now undermined warm, healthy interactions with women.

A third reason why listening for feelings is hard work for most of us is that *a speaker may take an emotional feeling and translate it up into a nonemotional idea.* He restates his feelings into thought concepts or "hints." Rather than saying, "I'm fearful of your traveling forty miles per hour on this narrow winding road," the person may say, "I noticed the speed limit is twenty-five miles per hour. Why are you going thirty-five?" Or, rather than saying, "I'm lonely; would you stay home tonight?" a wife says, "I think you should stay home tonight. You've already been out three nights this week."

The fourth reason that listening for feelings is difficult is that often *emotions do not exist in isolation.* They may be intertwined so that we may be experiencing two or more at the same time. For example, imagine that you are at home alone for the evening. You feel lonely. But as you think about the situation, you become aware that you are also angry because a friend stood you up for a reason that you believe was invalid. More reflection helps you see that you also have feelings of hopelessness because this has happened numerous times, and you know that it is a pattern in your friend's behavior that will not likely change.

Now I think you can see why "Step One: Listening for Feelings that Underlie Communication" is so difficult. Now let's move on to step two of this process.

Step 2: Reflecting the Perceived Feelings Back to the Speaker

The next step is to *reflect the perceived feelings back to the speaker.* Notice that I said *perceived.* Perceptive listening is an exercise in humility because we can never be certain that our perception of the emotion in another is accurate. *This is where we get into serious listening trouble.* We assume that our perception is accurate. And most people don't check out their perception with the authority—the other person.

This step is as crucial as the first. It is the only way the speaker knows if the listener is hearing the *full* communication and whether or not the message has been received accurately. Feeding back the perceived message to the speaker makes it possible for him to acknowledge whether or not he has been heard correctly.

Here's an illustration. If my child says, "I'm tired of this dumb homework. That stupid Mr. Barlow is always loading us with too much," my response might be, "You sound very discouraged doing your homework and angry with Mr. Barlow" (notice that I see the possibility of two emotions in this situation).

If I'm on target in identifying the feelings expressed and mirroring them back accurately, my child might respond, "Yeah, that's right. That's how I feel." If not, then he can clarify his feelings, and I can check out my perceptions again.

A second example might be helpful. A friend says, "What's the use? I try and try but I never can do it. No wonder I can't find a job. I'm a loser."

A helpful response might be, "I'm hearing you say that you feel hopeless. You feel trapped by failure. Is that what you're feeling?"

Let me reinforce something I've alluded to in this chapter. *Identify other people's feelings cautiously.* No one can be certain of what is going on inside another person. We may look at nonverbal cues and listen to the intensity and tone of voice, but there is a fifty-fifty

> •
> Identify other people's feelings cautiously.
> •

chance that we are wrong. And if we are wrong, our assumption will lead us down a wrong path that may destroy the opportunity to be a positive force in the individual's life. In addition, if that person has a grievance with me, my inaccurate response will more than likely lead us into more communication problems.

Let me say it again in another way: Don't assume that your perception of the person's emotions is correct. Check it out.

That being said, I still don't know of another area of communication that has been more rewarding to me than the act of listening for feelings. I still must discipline myself to practice this skill—especially in family relationships. But whenever I do, the results are gratifying. I feel that listening for feelings is one of the essential elements of effective interpersonal relationships. It is an integral element if love is to prosper within the Christian community.

Attitudes Shape the Outcome of Perceptive Listening

If we are going to develop the skill of listening for feelings, it is essential that we cultivate the proper attitude. Skillful listening for feelings is much more meaningful when it is infused with a compassionate, empathetic attitude. Let me describe several characteristics of the kind of attitude that will transform the process of listening for feelings into a significant expression of love.

First, *have a genuine desire to be helpful.* We listen intently because we want to help another person get in touch with what is festering inside. We're genuinely interested in knowing what feeling our friend is trying to express. In a world that often communicates indifference and hatred, we want to communicate the love of God within us—and we show it by listening.

Here's a second aspect of a helpful attitude: the best attitude is one of *a longing to hear the full communication*. The message of emotions is seldom easily heard. People usually don't scream, "I'm hurting!" Instead, they whisper it, in guarded statements, in test cases, to see if the environment is safe. Consequently, the perceptive listener will have to train his senses to discern what is being said.

When my son, Joel, was in junior high school, he participated in the school's wrestling program. One day he came home and announced decisively, "Dad, I'm quitting the team." I was surprised because I had received no earlier clues of his dissatisfaction. As Joel talked, I tried to practice the listening principles I've described in this chapter. After a while, Joel began to express disappointment that the coach did not praise his efforts. We talked more. Then Joel revealed his fear of going to the center of the floor before his teammates and putting his wrestling skills on the line. I heard feelings of fear, embarrassment, and disappointment. Together we talked through these feelings.

•

A helpful listener must provide an accepting, understanding environment.

•

Joel finished the year on the wrestling team. He made the decision himself, but I'm confident that the experience of talking out his inner turmoil in a supportive environment was a key factor in his decision to continue. What impressed me most about this experience was the fact that the *real* problems were hidden until they were revealed and faced through the talking-listening process.

A third piece of the listener's attitude is equally essential. *A helpful listener must provide an accepting, under-*

standing environment. Parents often lose excellent opportunities to support their children because they turn from understanding and acceptance to judgments, advice, threats, and so on. *This kind of attitude does not promote open, honest sharing.*

When someone is expressing negative emotions about us or our behavior, acceptance and understanding is especially difficult to practice. It seems unreasonable that I have to shelve my own feelings at the very time when I want to be understood—or make my point. However, a nondefensive posture on our part is a must. That approach will facilitate the expression of honest feelings in the other person and can lead to positive results. This doesn't mean that I will never get an opportunity to tell my story. But I recognize that *at this point,* I need to be the one who listens.

I can think of two examples of this kind of situation in my own life. As a parent, I have found it difficult to be accepting and understanding when my children express feelings of injustice or disagreement with me. Sometimes what I perceive as complaining or "belly-aching" seems irritating and unnecessary. Also, I have found it hard not to react defensively to church members who are not pleased with what I have done in my leadership capacity. In either of these situations, humbly listening to others as they expressed feelings against my actions was not easy. But I have found that such an attitude has been profitable for resolving the problem or conflict at hand.

Perceptive Listening Leads to Acceptance

The climate of acceptance is crucial to perceptive listening. What it will accomplish will delight you. For starters, acceptance releases people from fear of judgment and gives them permission to share honest feelings that have been troubling them. Many people are helped significantly through counseling when the counselor communicates an accepting, compassionate attitude. I have had people tell me that they have harbored feelings of defeat for years but never experienced the accepting, nonjudgmental environment which freed them to share.

Next, *acceptance nurtures a nondefensive environment.* This is critical, because people typically throw up barriers to their innermost feelings if they think they are being attacked or judged. Do you? But remember: *Acceptance is not to be equated with agreement.* Acceptance says, "I accept your feelings as valid to you. I do not condemn you for having them."

> •
> Acceptance is a significant way to express the love of Christ.
> •

Last, *acceptance is a significant way to express the love of Christ.* During his earthly ministry, Jesus lovingly and gently involved himself in troubled people's lives. When the Samaritan woman came to the well on a hot, dusty day, she met a person so different that she said, "How is it that You, being a Jew, ask me for a drink since I am a Samaritan woman?" (John 4:9 NASB). Then she began a dialogue with him that changed her life.

We, too, can be the same gracious, accepting individuals as our Lord. Through this compassionate spirit of understanding, the individuals we meet are freed to explore the inner needs, conflicts, and goals of their lives with a helping friend. They see modeled in us the loving concern of Christ.

> •
> Acceptance is important because our concept of God is shaped by the way others relate to us.
> •

Acceptance is important because our concept of God is shaped by the way others relate to us. Every so often I meet an individual who has developed a distorted view of God, and most of the time this distortion has come from faulty human models. An elderly woman once told me that she always felt God was stern and judgmental, that she could not feel from God the openness and acceptance she longed for. One of her parents had modeled this stern, judgmental attitude toward her, and the misconception she derived from her early experience had deeply influenced the way she had responded to God all her life. How much better to be living examples of the open love of Christ to those who need the kind of compassion he can provide!

Okay, But Can I Ever Give Advice?

Frequently during my workshops and seminars on listening someone will say, "You mean, all I can do is listen when I know the person is doing something wrong? That doesn't seem right. I need to straighten the person out. Isn't that an act of love?" If you are familiar with the Bible, you know that we *are* to offer counsel to the confused, correction to the erring, and even rebuke to the unrepentant sinner. The question is not whether or not such responses are appropriate—*it is a question of timing*.

Can you recall the counsel of James 1:19? He tells us that we are to be quick to listen and *slow to speak*. This is wise counsel that is too often violated. One of the most common problems associated with ineffective listening is the tendency to respond too quickly. In my judgment 90 percent of the time we give our opinion, advice, or counsel

- before we know all the facts
- before we know the real problem or need
- before the person is finished
- before the person is *ready* for help

Our well-intentioned help falls on deaf ears. If we don't rein in the impulse to fix the person, to straighten him or her out, to solve the problem, we'll accomplish little or nothing.

I said the issue is a question of timing. We try to short-circuit the process by giving our input *before the other person is mentally or emotionally ready.* Three steps are essential before you give advice.

Step 1: The speaker expresses the need to communicate emotions.

Step 2: The listener practices perceptive, nonjudgmental listening.

Step 3: The feeling is "talked out."

Steps 1 through 3 might take five to fifteen minutes. Only when step 3 is finished will the speaker be ready for input. Then step 4 is appropriate.

Step 4: The listener shares his or her perspective if needed or appropriate.

The sequence can be illustrated as follows:

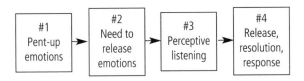

Keep this four-step sequence clear because the entire process can be short-circuited by a listener's tendency to advise, moralize, ridicule, or judge. Before solutions are discussed, the emotions must be adequately ventilated in a climate of acceptance. I have found that in the process, the speaker frequently works through his or her own constructive solutions without any "counsel." If I feel the need to share a biblical perspective or insight, I do it during the problem-solving segment that *follows* the feelings segment.

I recall a time when one of the members of our church came to see me to discuss a personal problem she was encountering at work. During the thirty to forty-five minutes we spent together, she poured out her frustration concerning the circumstances in which she found herself. As I listened I would occasionally express what I heard her saying, ask for clarification of a point, or encourage her to expand on some issue. At no time did I advise her or tell her what she should do.

I simply listened.

Yet as she prepared to leave, she said, "You've really helped me with the problem. Thanks a lot." In truth, I had been a catalyst that helped her solve her own problem.

Time to Reflect and Apply

I have said that listening for feelings is not an easy skill to master. Yet one of the most common problems in perceptive listening is the inability to listen for the emotions that underlie communication. It will be valuable for you to consider your own attitudes and skills in this area. The exercises that follow will assist you in this evaluation.

1. Checking Up on Yourself

Fill out the following self-check chart by circling the appropriate answer for each statement.

1. I have difficulty identifying my own feelings.	Never	Sometimes	Usually
2. I tend to concentrate on the content of another's message, rather than feelings.	Never	Sometimes	Usually
3. I identify others' emotions accurately.	Never	Sometimes	Usually
4. I respect others' feelings.	Never	Sometimes	Usually
5. When speaking, I identify my own emotions by name.	Never	Sometimes	Usually
6. I check out my perceptions of another's feelings.	Never	Sometimes	Usually
7. I can empathize when others express feelings.	Never	Sometimes	Usually

Remember the value of getting other people's perceptions. Ask someone to rate you in these seven areas of listening.

2. Weekly Journaling

In the coming week keep track of all situations you encounter in which you felt emotions. Name the emotion, the circumstances that prompted it, and how it influenced your communication. Do the same thing for the emotions that you are aware of in others. Try to be aware of situations in which you knew that emotions were present in the other person, but you were not certain what they were.

3. Going Further

The following two exercises will be valuable to you for further growth.

1. Review the list of emotions I've given you in this chapter.
   a. Photocopy them and post them in a place where you can review them frequently.
   b. As you interact and observe people, look for levels of intensity in emotions.
   c. This week, as you watch television, try to identify emotions in actors. Compare your response with someone else's.

2. What follows are a number of feeling statements to analyze. The fundamental question to answer about each is: "What feeling is the speaker expressing?" Use the emotions listed earlier in this chapter to help you but do not be limited to them.

When you have identified the feeling, jot down a response that reflects back to the speaker the feeling you think he or she is expressing. Remember, no *preaching, moralizing, advising,* or *ridiculing.*

Statement	Feeling(s) Being Expressed	Appropriate Response
"Teachers don't care! They load homework on us like we are slaves."		
"We won! And I got the winning hit."		
"You like Tom better than me, don't you?"		

Statement	Feeling(s) Being Expressed	Appropriate Response
"Couldn't you stay home tonight? I've been by myself every night this week."	_____ _____ _____	_____ _____ _____
"I can't ask her for a date. She'd never go out with me."	_____ _____ _____	_____ _____ _____
"I'm having a hard time studying the Bible, but I'm going to master it somehow."	_____ _____ _____	_____ _____ _____
"I made this all by myself; I think it's pretty."	_____ _____ _____	_____ _____ _____
"I should not have done it. You had a right to be mad at me."	_____ _____ _____	_____ _____ _____
"If he finds out, what'll I do? I've never been in trouble like this before."	_____ _____ _____	_____ _____ _____
"Jim said I'd make sales if I did what he said. Today I sold three units. I think maybe I'll be able to do it."	_____ _____ _____	_____ _____ _____
"I hate Sunday school. Mrs. Waters is the most boring teacher I've ever had. Why do you make me go?"	_____ _____ _____	_____ _____ _____

CHAPTER FIVE

[Listening to Learn]

•

What you have said I will consider. What you have to say I will with patience hear and find a time both meet to hear and answer such high things.

William Shakespeare, *Julius Caesar*, Act I, Scene 2

Does not the ear test words as the tongue tastes food?

Job 12:11

A time came several years ago when I had to get serious about physical exercise. The summer days in Phoenix, Arizona, where I live, are blistering hot, so I like to get

87

up before sunrise to hike because it's cooler then (during August in Phoenix, "cooler" is a relative term!). I've come to treasure the early morning when the city is still asleep and quiet walks are a way to prepare for the day.

During my early morning exercise, I often thank God for his abundant blessings: a healthy, coordinated body that functions smoothly; energy to be productive through the day; and a mind that is stimulated by new ideas, visions, and opportunities.

One of the best ways I can express my gratitude for my mind is by developing it. In fact, the writer of Hebrews comments that individuals who "by constant use have trained themselves to distinguish good from evil" have the mark of maturity (Heb. 5:14). The words "constant use" are more literally translated "exercise." We train our minds by exercising them so that we can more carefully distinguish between good and evil. What a foundation for wisdom!

In this chapter we are going to focus on the element of perceptive listening that will help us to learn—listening for ideas.

We listen for ideas because we ourselves have a problem or need. We require input from someone else, and we listen to receive the data that another person possesses. For example, if I feel that my schedule is getting out of control, I may go to hear a lecture by a time management expert. Or I may consult with a colleague about a personality conflict with which I am struggling.

Beware of Those Internal Listening Filters!

How the speaker and the listener relate to each other can be of great significance in the process of listening for ideas. A weak or injured relationship creates a situation in which listening filters are apt to be present. *Lis-*

tening filters are internal processes that cause a listener to omit or distort information, to inaccurately receive what is being communicated. Such filters may be unique to a single relationship or related to certain groups—gender, age, ethnic, and so on. Frequently listening filters are deeply rooted biases or prejudices that we have learned in our childhood or youth.

I know a man who had great difficulty listening to women. He might appear to listen, but it was really a front. He told me that as far back as he could remember, he had assumed that women didn't have anything important to say, so he spent little time or effort listening to them. You can imagine how his wife felt when she wanted to talk with him.

You might think you don't have such biases, but you could be wrong. Here are three questions to ask yourself. The answers will help you determine whether listening filters are present in a particular situation, and predict how these filters may distort the information the speaker is sharing.

Question 1: What is my attitude toward the speaker? Do I feel positive or negative toward him? Any of the following factors may influence how we feel about a given speaker:

Political persuasion
Gender
Race or nationality
Religious convictions
Age
Social standing
Physical appearance
Educational background
Geographical location
Lifestyle

I've never met anyone who didn't have some kind of bias that influenced his or her listening abilities, though it was often in ways the person didn't realize or want to acknowledge. I've had to admit that I have some in my own life. I recall my first close encounter with black Christians. I had not been aware of any prejudice toward blacks until a black community invited me to join them. Suddenly I became very anxious. Until I resolved the fears and misconceptions that were causing my anxiety, they threatened to influence my ability to listen to members of this group.

> •
> ### Listening filters can be subtle.
> •

Listening filters can be subtle. Because someone uses a Bible translation others have criticized, we may tend to discredit all that the speaker is saying. Do we close our ears when someone from a "liberal" group begins to speak? Do we assume someone who describes himself or herself as a "fundamentalist" has nothing important to say?

Another subtle filter is the look-alike filter. If the speaker reminds us of a neighbor whom we couldn't tolerate, we may find ourselves disinterested in the speaker. Or the person may have personality characteristics similar to someone we admire. So we perk up, thinking, "This person is going to be great!" Unfortunately, this may happen unconsciously; we may not realize that the basis for how we listen is unsound.

Question 2: Who has conditioned me? Often we have been conditioned for or against a speaker by what others have said: "I hope you like him. I found him boring." "You got Dr. Bonedry for Biology. I pity you!" "She's a neat person. You'll like her as a counselor. She helped me a lot."

I recall a college friend who signed up for a class taught by a godly professor who had a poor reputation as a teacher. My friend told me, "Norm, I'm determined to go into the class believing that this man has much to teach me. I refuse to be conditioned against him by others." Toward the end of the semester, we were in a conversation in which that prof's name came up. My friend said that he had found many helpful insights from the teacher. Perhaps his refusal to be prejudiced by fellow students was a deciding factor.

A counselor friend once told me of a lady who came to him describing her husband as a barbarous brute—unreasonable, disgusting, and uncooperative. When the husband came for counseling, my friend was amazed to find the man was a cooperative, "civilized" person. My friend had been led to believe something inconsistent with later facts.

Question 3: What are my expectations? What information do I expect to receive from this person? A friend of mine attended a conference for her personal enrichment. The literature she received and the comments of friends who were familiar with the speakers had led her to expect a stimulating and helpful experience. After the conference she said, "Because my expectations were not met in some seminars, I found it difficult to pay attention to certain speakers. I expected them to be stimulating and creative in their presentations, but I discovered they were repeating what they had written in their books. It turned me off." Being aware of our expectations can help us realize when they influence our listening. If expectations are not being met, perhaps they can be adjusted to achieve realistic benefits and to make the best of the situation for all involved.

Make Sharing Rewarding

I grew up a shy, insecure young man. When I was in the Navy, stationed in Norfolk, Virginia, the pastor of my church asked me to preach the sermon on "Youth Sunday." The very idea terrified me, but whether I was naive or foolish, I agreed. That was the beginning of my training to preach. I struggled to communicate the Word of God effectively. I'd pray, plead, and prepare diligently for a particular sermon, and then stand before my audience with fear and trembling, desperately desiring their encouragement and acceptance. As I gazed at my audience, I was struck by the lack of response. The "stone faces" I encountered only heightened my uneasiness as I preached before them. Actually they were wonderfully gracious people who loved me, but to this unsure novice it was a humbling learning experience.

One day during this period in my life, I was reading my Bible, and the Spirit of God encouraged my heart. I read of the young man Jeremiah's encouragement from the Lord. Jeremiah appeared to have experienced what I was encountering. As I read his prayer, it echoed the thoughts and feelings I was experiencing. Here are Jeremiah's words:

> Then I said, "Alas, Lord God! Behold I do not know how to speak, because I am a youth."
>
> Jeremiah 1:6 NASB

Our Lord, being the absolute best perceptive listener, heard the young man's cry and answered him. Listen to his words of encouragement:

> But the LORD said to me, "Do not say, 'I am a youth,' because everywhere I send you, you shall go, and all that I command you, you shall speak. Do not be afraid of them, for I am with you to deliver you."
>
> verses 7–8 NASB

As the years have rolled by, I have come to see that listeners have great power to encourage or discourage, build up or tear down those who speak. In the process, they may make the act of listening more pleasurable since an encouraged speaker is a more relaxed, personable, and interesting speaker.

Recently I sat in a classroom as a devoted young man named Terry started teaching the Bible. After about five minutes of lecturing, he stopped, sighed, and said, "I am very nervous. I am new at this and find it very difficult." As a listener, I had found his biblical insights thoughtful, but Terry needed feedback that would affirm his strengths and encourage him to go on. Fortunately, this happened, and Terry is developing into a fine Bible teacher.

You, the listener, can do many things to facilitate the process of sharing ideas:

Determine to look attentive and eager. A pleasant look encourages a speaker. The powerful preacher Charles H. Spurgeon once said, "To me it is an annoyance if even a blind man does not look me in the face." Whether we are sitting across the table while a friend tells of an irritating problem he is trying to resolve or listening while the manager shares company goals, our attentiveness will enhance the communication process.

Express appreciation verbally. Affirmative responses, like "What you said was helpful," "Thanks for sharing," or "I'd never heard that concept before, but it's exactly what I needed to resolve my problem," encourage individuals to continue speaking. A person who sees his ideas as worthwhile and appreciated will be motivated to share more. If you appreciate what a speaker says, tell them!

Participate with the speaker. Participation may be either verbal or nonverbal. Verbal participation includes raising questions or making comments. It may be a simple statement such as "I agree," "yes," or "That's helpful." Nonverbal participation may include a smile, a nod of approval, or an attentive look. All of these express interest in what the speaker is communicating.

Don't interrupt. Interrupting inhibits the flow of the speaker's thoughts and communicates "I don't want to listen to you." For some listeners, not interrupting may require developing the self-discipline that makes it possible to wait until the other person is finished before speaking. Such a person also may need to check their habit of planning a response rather than attending to the speaker.

How We Distort the Message

When we listen, we alter what we hear to make it fit our way of thinking, our present knowledge, and our past experiences. If we are aware of this subconscious process, we will be less likely to distort the message. The following three principles will help you process information more accurately.

Principle #1. We tend to manipulate the speaker's information to fit our perceptions. As another individual speaks to us, we take the data and assimilate it into our present values, biases, opinions, and needs. This process usually goes on without any conscious effort on our part.

One result of this is that we may alter the facts or meaning that the speaker intended. Then, when we report to a third person what the speaker said, we give a different slant to it that is inaccurate. Imagine, for example, that you as a wife are conveying to your child a message from your husband. Your husband's message was "Tell Billy that I want him to mow the lawn this afternoon." However, you are concerned because you know that Billy has a tendency to put things off. Thus your message is "Your dad called and said that he wanted you to mow the lawn *right now*. You'll be in trouble if he comes home and it's not done!" You have assimilated your personal concerns into your husband's message. Billy may interpret your words to mean that his father is angry with him. All he wanted to communicate was that Billy should mow the lawn that afternoon.

Principle #2. We condense and simplify the message to remember it more easily. Speakers usually fail to consider that we cannot hear, assimilate, and store a lot of information quickly. In casual conversation the communication process moves back and forth with short, digestible bits of information. Sometimes, however, when we are purposefully giving information that we want others to remember, or convey to others, we speak in longer time units, giving much more information. We forget that no one can retain all the details that we are giving.

•

Speakers usually fail to consider that we cannot hear, assimilate, and store a lot of information quickly.

•

Preachers and Bible teachers consistently violate this principle. They speak uninterrupted for thirty to forty minutes and then assume that the congregation heard, understood, assimilated, and stored the data. No way! Often when someone asks about a sermon I heard, I stop, scratch my head as though that would prime the pump, and finally say, "He talked about some Old Testament prophet. I think it was Haggai, but I'm not sure."

Perceptive listeners discipline themselves to gather as much input as possible. They learn to interact mentally with the speaker's ideas. They develop the habit of jotting down notes, including key points or questions they want to ask. They are observant of nonverbal cues that help them gain the fullest understanding from the speaker. If appropriate, they may ask the speaker to slow down, to clarify information, or to give practical examples.

Principle #3. We focus our attention on the element that appeals to or impresses us, and then we let our imagination run free to embellish those parts of the message. We may expand on some aspect of the speaker's ideas that we agreed with and ignore what we judged unimportant. The ironic thing is that what we have chosen to embellish may have been incidental to what the speaker intended. He would be disappointed that we so misrepresented what he had intended to communicate. If I were listening to a speaker who mentioned something about antique sports cars, I'd be sorely tempted to begin thinking about a Triumph TR2 that I'd restored, or an Austin Healy I've always admired. Whatever the speaker said for the next three to five minutes might be lost to me!

Principle #4. We listen for what we want or expect to hear. If I want permission from you to do something, I listen to hear that permission. Then I interpret what you say to fit what I want to hear. This occurs in both negative and positive situations. For example, if I am a likeable, permissive individual, you are more likely to hear me give permission, or agreement, whether I did or not. "Norm thinks like I do, so I know what he means." However, if you and I have had a negative relationship, you will likely hear my words as negative communication. You might think, "When Norm said that I speak often, he was implying that I am mouthy and should shut up," while I intended no negative connotation. I was really trying to say that you felt free to express your opinions.

The four principles that I have described help us understand how we typically alter data that we hear. It is a natural tendency. With that reality before us, we are challenged to develop a strategy that minimizes the danger of miscommunication.

Guidelines for Listening

I spoke earlier about the Hebrews 5:14 concept of training our senses so that we become more discerning people. In this book we are considering how to train our sense of hearing to gain the maximum benefit. One aspect of this is to sharpen our ability to listen for ideas. The following guidelines will assist you in this process.

Prepare Spiritually

Spiritual preparation is foundational for good listening; heart preparation through prayer opens us up to the resources of the Holy Spirit. Setting aside time to listen to God is helpful in preparing for listening.

Prepare Physically

Physical preparation is another essential for listening. Physical weariness, hunger, or thirst can decrease mental alertness and hamper listening. Sometimes we need rest or food before we're prepared to listen. It is valid to ask to postpone important communication until you are in a better frame of mind. Usually a brief, uninterrupted fifteen-minute rest renews us.

Prepare Mentally

Mental preparation is necessary too. Often we are loaded down with many other concerns. These thoughts, concerns, and emotions may be vying for attention and need to be put aside. That's not always easy to do, but we can develop skill in this area. Also, we need to know ahead of time what information we will need and what we should listen for.

Prepare Environmentally

Finally, environmental preparation is profitable. What location would be best for the discussion? Where could we listen with the least distraction? Do we habitually sit in the back of the auditorium where all those in front of us can distract us? When we listen in a one-to-one relationship, do we find a location which is private and comfortable and which allows us to have eye contact with the person speaking?

Use Analytical Skills

Use analytical skills to supplement listening. Our friends may need to learn how to think actively along with the speaker and to analyze the data the speaker is providing. A word of caution: Becoming too analytical can keep a listener from hearing what is being said. He may become so involved in his own thought processes that he misses important information.

Take Notes

Take notes on key points. It can help to jot down key information that comes out in discussions. It helps to make brief notes of essential ideas we don't want to forget; doing this aids in keeping information before us. But I emphasize *key* information. Taking elaborate notes can also distract a listener from what the speaker is saying. Many of us have learned that growth is a slow process. It's easy to get discouraged when we don't see the progress we hoped for. But we gain so much when we are persistent and develop our listenability. Then we learn from the information available to us. By practicing the concepts outlined in this chapter, we can listen more effectively for ideas.

Time to Reflect and Apply

To gain practical benefits from this chapter, it is important to apply the concepts to your listening relationships. The activities on the following pages are designed to help you in the process.

1. Checking Up on Yourself

Work through the following items to evaluate your ability to listen for ideas.

1. When I listen for information, I know what I'm listening for. Never Sometimes Usually

2. I am able to monitor my attitude toward the speaker. Never Sometimes Usually

3. I recognize who influences the data I hear. Never Sometimes Usually

4. I am in touch with how I tend to alter information I hear. Never Sometimes Usually

5. I prepare myself to hear important information.	Never	Sometimes	Usually
6. I take notes to help discipline my listening information.	Never	Sometimes	Usually

Remember to have someone rate you on these six areas.

2. Weekly Journaling

In the coming week keep a record of the following issues:

- Who and what influences the way I process information?
- What type of people do I have difficulty listening to and learning from?
- What am I aware of concerning how I listen to people's ideas and information?
- What skills do I need to work on?

3. Going Further

The following exercises will continue to stimulate growth in listening for information.

1. Review the statements under "Checking Up on Yourself" in this chapter. Which of these factors influences how you receive information from a speaker? List the people with whom you have significant relationships. How do these factors shape what you hear from those people?
2. Listen to a five-minute news report on the radio with a friend. Then compare your perceptions of

what was said. To make this even more interesting, tape-record the news report, compare your perceptions, and then listen again to the tape.

3. Circle the following situation(s) where you practice the skill described:

I consciously *prepare* myself to listen in
    study groups
    Sunday school class
    sermons
    news reports
    other _____

I concentrate on the speaker as a *communicator* in
    study groups
    Sunday school class
    sermons
    news reports
    other _____

I give feedback effectively when possible in
    study groups
    Sunday school class
    sermons
    news reports
    other _____

I *actively* think along with the speaker, using *analytical skills* in
    study groups
    Sunday school class
    sermons
    news reports
    other _____

I jot down *notes* of key ideas I want to remember in
  study groups
  Sunday school class
  sermons
  news reports
  other _____

CHAPTER SIX

[The Remarkable Question]

•

The question is a remarkable conversation instrument. When used skillfully it can point the way to the solution of a problem. It can give an individual insight into his own feeling and motivations or into those of another person. It can arouse a mind from its inertia and set it into motion.[1]

Jesse Nirenberg

"Who do people say the Son of Man is?"
Matthew 16:13

"But what about you?" he asked. "Who do you say I am?"
Matthew 16:15

Questions are powerful tools in the hands of a skilled communicator. This deceptively simple device has the power to capture and dominate another person's thought processes—pointing out deficiencies; leading into new pathways of thought; probing motives, attitudes, and prejudices. I read somewhere that a child can ask a thousand questions that the wisest man cannot answer. Even a child can profoundly challenge our thinking. The listener who knows how to ask insightful questions will gain more valuable data and thus be more discerning—more perceptive.

There once were two golfers, Bart and Len, who were competing in a tournament. They came to the eighteenth hole with their scores tied. Len looked at Bart and asked, "Do you take a breath before or after you swing?" Bart lost the tournament because Len's question prompted him to focus on his breathing rather than his swing. He was defeated by a well-timed question.

Let me demonstrate this power on you. What is the sixth book of the Old Testament? Now try to dismiss the question from your mind without answering it. Chances are you won't be able to do it. Something in your thought process pushes you to respond. You cannot leave it unanswered, even though you know the question is unimportant.

I have never forgotten an incident that happened to me over twenty-five years ago. I was near the completion of a master's program at Wheaton College. Dr. Lois Lebar was my faculty advisor. On this particular day I was in her office discussing my thesis, which she had supervised. During our conversation she asked me what I planned to do when I graduated.

"I'm motivated to go into teaching at the college level," I replied.

"Do you think you're ready?" she asked.

The question caught me off guard. I assumed she would say, "Wonderful, I'm sure you'll be an outstanding teacher." Instead, she planted a question in my mind that persisted in my thoughts as I left her office: "Am I ready?" I knew that Dr. Lebar was exceptionally skilled at asking thought-provoking questions, but that day I felt the impact of one on my own life. She made me a believer in the power of an effective question.

It's my turn to ask *you* three questions.

1. Are you committed to being a more effective listener?
2. Do you want to reap the fruit of perceptive listening?
3. Are you willing to pay the price it costs to learn this skill?

If your answers are "yes," then you'll want to develop skill in the effective use of questions. Let me say again that questions are powerful tools. They carry the power to probe the speaker's thoughts, keep him involved in a dialogue, and guide his thoughts in a profitable direction.

Why Do Questions Fail?

My opening comments stressed the power of questions. I said that I place a high value on their potential. Yet often they don't live up to this potential. When they are posed with little thought or skill, they fall into disgrace and disuse. When used unwisely or carelessly, the question is robbed of its power. Thus we need to ask ourselves, "What causes questions to lose their power and become ineffective?"

•

Questions lose their power when they are poorly worded.

•

Questions lose their power when they are *poorly worded*. That's because poorly worded questions create confusion. I recall a fellow graduate student who struggled with the use of questions. He would state his question. Then he would explain and embellish the question until we were sufficiently confused and unable to answer it. I soon learned that answering my friend's questions was impossible because it was too difficult to find out what he wanted to know!

Questions also lose their power when they are *the wrong kind*. The most powerful questions are those that affect our lives. Wrong questions are those which pursue irrelevant material and lead others down dead-end streets. Effective listeners ask questions that are designed to aid the speaker—not satisfy the listener's curiosity.

> •
> The most powerful
> questions are those
> that affect our lives.
> •

When the *question is answered by the speaker*, the question loses its potential to initiate thought. I once had a Sunday school teacher who would ask questions but never gave us time to respond. This practice both irritated and frustrated me; it also caused me to lose interest in his questions because I knew he wouldn't let me get actively involved.

Some questions are weak and anemic because they are *thoughtless*. Powerful questions are carefully chosen. Through practice, wise questions can be formed quickly. Some listeners might find it helpful to have a pad of paper handy to jot down questions that arise. Then they can be reviewed before they are posed. Just this morning I was teaching at a conference center. I had decided to end my presentation with three questions that would help the audience apply key biblical principles to their own lives. I thought a long time about which questions would be most helpful to my listeners. I had many that I could ask, but I had to

> •
> Powerful questions
> are carefully chosen.
> •

find the three that would most effectively motivate the people in attendance to positive actions.

If *too many* questions are used, they lose their impact. They can make others feel uncomfortable and defensive, as though they were being grilled. Remember my conversation with Dr. Lebar? She asked only one question, but it was relevant, clear, and direct. I went away with it hooked into my brain like a barb. She had identified one pivotal question that would challenge my thinking, and that one question caused genuine soul searching in me.

> •
> Too many questions can make others feel uncomfortable and defensive.
> •

In everyday conversation people want to enter into dialogue with each other. Most of us don't want to listen to a monologue. We appreciate a relaxed environment that has give and take.

Questions should be interspersed with personal sharing, so that each conversational partner feels that he is sharing of himself. If the individual senses that he is being grilled, or that the conversation is one-sided, he will be more likely to close down and withdraw.

Making Questions Our Friends

When skillfully used, the question is a versatile device, able to serve many useful functions. It can benefit us in six ways. First, it can help us *get clarification from a speaker*: "I'm uncertain about what you meant when you said 'I'm ambivalent.' Could you clarify that for me?" Questions such as these cue the speaker in to any confusion and let him know when to pause and explain more carefully.

Second, questions *enable listeners to reflect back on what they have heard*. This helps the speaker and the listener match their perceptions to see if they are on the same track. In an upcoming chapter, I will talk to you about the importance of finding a shared meaning. The key to accomplishing this is using reflective questions to feed back the essential words of the message: "I'm hearing you say that you are discouraged with your poor sales record. Is that correct?" When we give feedback on what we're hearing, the other person can affirm or correct what we've reflected in our question.

•

Questions can build relationships by helping us gather essential information for mutual problem solving.

•

Third, questions are an invaluable *help in collecting vital information.* They help us find out facts we need to discover about the other person or the problem before us. Questions like these can build relationships by helping us gather essential information for mutual problem solving.

In our church family gatherings, we frequently use questions as a means of helping Christians learn about each other. Questions initiate conversations that lead to personal sharing. In this way, we grow in our knowledge of one another. This practice has helped break down barriers of alienation and has enabled fellow Christians to discover common interests that enrich their relationships.

It's important to recognize that questions can be placed on a continuum from high-structured to low-structured. A highly structured question is used to gain specific information: "What is your favorite food?" Low-structured questions seek more general information and invite the speaker to share more freely: "How have your parents' attitudes toward food influenced you?" Notice that the low-structured question gives the responder much more freedom to reply in a variety of ways. Low-structured questions are likely to produce more information.

The fourth way questions can serve us is by *helping us confront another person.* Jesus used a confronting question when he asked Nicodemus, "Are you Israel's teacher . . . and do not understand these things?" (John 3:10). We may phrase questions to confront an individual either directly or indirectly. A direct question might be "Why did you lie to me about where you were?" A more indirect question might be "I felt upset when I found you'd lied to me. Can we talk about it?" Indirect questions will probably get at the same issue but may be less threatening to the other person.

•

Provocative questions
motivate others
to more serious
thought.

•

Questions are invaluable for a fifth reason. *They serve well in stimulating the spirit of inquiry.* Provocative questions motivate others to more serious thought. When we use questions wisely, we are able to guide the thinking of an individual or group; we hold the initiative. As a matter of fact, we can *control* the group process by the skillful use of questions.

Used in a negative way, questions can put another on the defensive—have you ever felt backed into a corner by someone's persistent questions? My emphasis here is intended to be positive. The wise question is like a rudder on a ship; it directs the flow of thought and conversation.

•

Effective questions
can stimulate growth.

•

Here's one final reason I encourage the skillful use of questions: they are a great way to *lead people to apply truth and clarify values.* Effective questions can stimulate growth. That's what Dr. Lebar was doing when she posed the question to me about my readiness to teach. Another powerful illustration is found in the life of Jesus Christ. In Matthew 16:13–16, Jesus raises two questions to his disciples:

> When Jesus came to the region of Caesarea Philippi, he asked his disciples, "Who do people say the Son of Man is?"
> They replied, "Some say John the Baptist; others say Elijah; and still others, Jeremiah or one of the prophets."
> "But what about you?" he asked. "Who do you say I am?"
> Simon Peter answered, "You are the Christ, the Son of the living God."

In raising these two simple but powerful questions, Jesus led Peter to verbalize his faith that Jesus was the Messiah. No doubt this was the first time Peter had verbalized his growing conviction.

Questions are one of the most effective ways to help people look at their values. They challenge commonly accepted ideas and force the individual to defend what he holds dear. When we use questions for the purpose of values clarification, we attempt to aid an individual in examining or articulating his or her personal beliefs.

Questions are also a fundamental tool in helping individuals apply new concepts to their lives. "What would be the first step in applying this principle to your life?" "If you were to practice this teaching, what changes would you make?" Questions like these have the potential to initiate change in the individual.

Can you see why I count the question as one of my close friends? Perhaps you see why Nirenberg said, "The question is a remarkable conversation instrument." Why not consider anew how this provocative tool can help you as a communicator? What new strength could it contribute to your interpersonal skills?

Guidelines for the Questioner

I have said that questions are ineffective when used carelessly, but invaluable when used carefully, wisely, and skillfully. If we want questions to serve us, we must treat them with the dignity that gives them power. To do so, it will be helpful to investigate several guidelines for the effective use of questions:

Phrase questions simply, directly, and clearly. Observe Christ's use of questions. They are remarkably simple, pointedly direct, and very clear:

"How can Satan drive out Satan?" (Mark 3:23)
"Who are my mother and my brothers?" (Mark 3:33)
"Why are you so afraid? Do you still have no faith?"
(Mark 4:40)
"Are your hearts hardened?" (Mark 8:17)
"What did Moses command you?" (Mark 10:3)
"What do you want me to do for you?" (Mark 10:36)

Notice how concise these questions are. Recently, I've been coaching an adult Sunday school teacher. This man is diligent in studying the Bible and demonstrates a number of characteristics of strong teaching. But I noticed that when he asks questions of the class, they look confused and dazed, and an awkward period of silence follows. Thus we've been working on writing out clear and simple questions. The change in class participation is already noticeable.

Many people assume that anyone can ask an effective question without practice. Not true! For several years I instructed seminary students in teaching methods. I found the students consistently weak in phrasing good questions until they practiced applying the principles of simplicity, directness, and clarity. So the odds are you will strengthen the effectiveness of your questions if you write them out before asking them. Then chop out needless phrases. Simplify them. Make them easy to grasp the first time they are heard.

When you are involved as a listener, *think carefully* about the question that you want to ask. Will it get the information you want? Will it entice the other person to think more deeply?

Start conversations with easy questions. Use questions that the other person does not have to think deeply about. The first couple of minutes of a relationship are the most awkward; using questions that invite a ready response gives the other person confidence and helps him relax.

A good principle is to begin conversations with questions that are low-structured and then move to high-structured ones if you need specific data as the relationship becomes established. Since the low-structured question gives the speaker more freedom of response, he is more likely to relax and feel comfortable. This is true whether we are meeting new friends, interviewing someone for a job, or establishing initial rapport with a counselee. Ask questions like, "Could you tell me more about . . . how you felt, why he yelled, or what prompted you to . . . ?" "What would you have done to change it?"

Use "yes" and "no" questions sparingly. Such questions do not tend to involve the person significantly or to stimulate creative inquiry. Neither do they usually provide us with any significant insight. If we are trying to gain information about the individual with whom we are speaking, we will use questions that encourage him or her to share more fully.

Also be cautious about asking "why" questions. When focusing on interpersonal problems, "why" questions often give little or no help in resolving the problem. Asking "Why did you do it?" may not be as helpful as asking "What could we do to resolve the problem?" or "What are you willing to do to establish a healthier relationship with your sister?" The "why" questions often are less solution oriented than "what" or "how" questions.

> •
> The "why" questions often are less solution oriented than "what" or "how" questions.
> •

Practice answering a question with a question. It may be flattering to hear another say "Will you do this for me?" But it may be more helpful to respond, "What do you see as the first step?" and then to guide the individual in working through the solution himself. A principle I have tried to apply is never to do for the other person what he can *more profitably* do for himself. This applies to answering questions. If it is more profitable for the other person to think, analyze, and inquire, then we should consider the profit of answering his questions with a question.

"Before I answer, I'd like to know what you think."
"How would you answer the question?"
"How would the rest of you respond to Jo's question?"

An underlying conviction of this book is that listening can be a ministry for the Christian. The wise listener wants to respond to the speaker in a way that will promote that person's growth and insight. In some cases, answering a question with a question may be the most appropriate means of reaching this goal. This is especially true when the person to whom we are relating has a habit of allowing others to do his thinking for him.

Our goal can be to excite him about the challenge of personal discovery.

Once we have asked the question, it is important to allow ample time for the individual—or group—to respond. Many people become nervous or impatient if their questions are not answered immediately. But silence is an indication that someone is thinking! If the question is worth asking, it is worth allowing the person to whom it is asked an opportunity to ponder his or her response.

> • The wise listener wants to respond to the speaker in a way that will promote that person's growth and insight. •

In a group situation, ask the question first and then direct it to an individual. This tactic keeps the entire group involved. When only one individual is questioned, others may turn off their thought processes: "He's asking Jeff. I can relax and not think about it."

Avoid questions that attack. Questions can be used to ridicule, attack, embarrass, or belittle.

"Don't you know any better than to do that?"

"Why did you do such a foolish thing?"

"Don't you realize a Christian shouldn't think such thoughts?"

Such questions can do damage to the person and cause him to withdraw from interaction. But our purpose in questioning should always be to build up and edify the other person—not tear him down.

An excellent biblical principle is contained in Ephesians 4:29: "Do not let any unwholesome talk come out of your mouths, but only what is helpful for building others up according to their needs, that it may benefit those who listen." We are challenged to make all of our speech positive, constructive, and wholesome. Every expression from our lips can be a ministry of the indwelling Spirit. The questions we ask others are a valuable means of applying the principle contained in this verse.

Developing Questioning Skills

Anyone can learn to use questions skillfully. But it requires two essential commitments. First, the individual must be committed to healthy attitudes that are conducive to being an effective questioner. Remember, attitudes lead to actions. If my attitude is "I'm the smartest person here. Everyone should listen to me," then I will not care about asking questions.

Earlier in this book I spoke about the importance of the attitude of humility for perceptive listening. Humility cultivates a servant's heart. Humility leads me to ask, "How can I draw out the thoughts and feelings in this other person?"

The second essential commitment is that I am going to practice the skills basic to effective questioning. Those skills are contained in this chapter. As you finish reading, you will be challenged to apply what you've learned. You have to decide if this is important enough that it is worth the discipline required to master the skills.

Time to Reflect and Apply

I have stressed the need to use questions effectively. The exercises that follow will help you apply what you have been learning.

1. Checking Up on Yourself

Work through the following statements as a means of giving yourself feedback.

1. I consider asking questions an important part of interpersonal relationships.   Never   Sometimes   Usually

2. I can phrase questions in a clear, simple, and direct manner.   Never   Sometimes   Usually

3. I use questions to draw others out and gain understanding of their ideas, issues, etc.   Never   Sometimes   Usually

4. I use "yes" and "no" questions sparingly.   Never   Sometimes   Usually

5. I don't use questions to attack, intimidate, or embarrass others.   Never   Sometimes   Usually

6. Others have told me that I ask helpful questions.   Never   Sometimes   Usually

7. I ask individuals what words mean as they use them.   Never   Sometimes   Usually

2. Weekly Journaling

During the coming week regularly reflect and write about the following:

- I would be more effective in asking questions if I . . .
- A person who could help me grow in this area is . . .
- One skill I want to practice today is . . .
- I will do it by . . .

3. *Going Further*

Read each question carefully. Decide whether it is effective or ineffective. Circle the ineffective questions. Beside them, jot down *why* they are ineffective (too long, too complex, attack the speaker, poorly worded, nonstimulating, etc.). Try to rewrite them to make them more effective.

1. "Al, if this questioning business is important, and I'm sure it is, should we elaborate on those factors which facilitate direct bridges to more skillful wording or just better sentences?"
2. "You're not feeling well?"
3. "Why should John stay home and you get to go? Is that fair?"
4. "What in this chapter could be misconstrued as being an apparent attack upon the reliability of the reader to assimilate verbal content?"
5. "Apparently you've made up your mind to have your own way—right?"
6. "Should every Christian pray?"
7. "Does John 17 indicate that it is more important to stand or kneel when praying?"
8. "What have I been doing that's aggravated your anger toward me?"
9. "Would you expand on point three? It's still unclear."
10. "Why don't you sell your car to pay the debt?"
11. "You think you're better than I am, don't you?"
12. "I'm upset. Could we talk about this later?"

CHAPTER SEVEN

[Clarifying the Message]

•

An official who must listen to the pleas of his clients should listen patiently and without rancor, because a petitioner wants attention to what he says even more than the accomplishing of that for which he came.[1]

Ptahhotep, an Egyptian Pharaoh

Do two walk together unless they have agreed to do so?

Amos 3:3

A close friend, I'll call her Sue, told me of an incident that happened during Bible study. Her friend Molly was sharing her interpretation of a passage of Scripture. Sue felt the explanation was very philosophical and difficult to grasp. With an upward sweep of her hand, she told Molly, "Your ideas are too heady!" Later Molly told Sue that she was offended by that term because she interpreted the statement to mean that her ideas were of no value. It created a problem for Molly and forced her to confront Sue with her feelings. Thankfully they were able to understand what Sue meant and what Molly heard.

This incident reminds us how easy it is to send messages with mixed meanings. The risk of being misunderstood increases when little or no opportunity is given for dialogue, feedback, and clarification. When there is an opportunity to clarify the speaker's ideas and check the accuracy of what has been heard, your communication is enhanced and your relationships can grow.

The Shared-Meaning Process

One concept my wife and I have found especially valuable in our relationship is what experts call "reaching a shared meaning." We learned it several years ago as participants in a communication workshop. I am convinced that it is one of the most basic—and crucial—concepts necessary for healthy interpersonal communication.

Shared meaning is the process by which two individuals test what is being discussed to see if they both have the same understanding. Because meanings are in people not in words, the same word can have two totally different meanings. Consider the statement, "Don't be late for supper." "Late" can mean fifteen minutes to the person who is preparing the meal; whereas, it can mean an hour to the person who is arriving for the meal. I know of a businessman who never arrives at meetings on time because he believes that they never start until fifteen minutes has passed. So he considers himself to be on time when he is fifteen minutes late!

Why Is Coming to Shared Meaning Important?

At first the process of coming to a shared meaning may seem artificial, but there are several benefits that are gained by using it. First, it increases the likelihood that what the speaker says and what the listener understands will be the same message. The process forces both speaker and listener to stay with the dialogue long enough to achieve an accurate perception. Step by step, mutual understanding is achieved.

Second, it challenges the listener to become intently involved in what the speaker is saying. A person who knows he is working toward a shared meaning realizes that he has to repeat the message back, so he listens more carefully.

Third, it can increase speaking and listening skills. Typical conversations have little or no monitoring processes to check on the accuracy of communication. The shared-meaning process is a self-imposed discipline to monitor how well and how accurately two people communicate. Both speaker and listener are required to contribute their skills to the process.

> •
> A person who knows he is working toward a shared meaning realizes that he has to repeat the message back, so he listens more carefully.
> •

When to Use the Process

When should this process be used? It's most useful when the *message* is vital to a relationship, when there is danger of a misunderstanding, or when one person is fearful that his or her message will be heard incorrectly.

121

These topics might relate to financial matters, in-law relationships, rearing children, to name just a few. The persons involved in each situation will have to decide what concerns are especially significant to them.

Think back to a time when you felt misunderstood by someone or when you heard someone close to you say, "You've got it all wrong; that's not what I said!" The shared-meaning process might have aided you in coming to a common understanding.

The positive benefit this process offers makes the discipline it requires worthwhile. You might consider using it with your coworkers, children, friends, and parents.

"Checking Out" the Words

The shared-meaning process is rooted in a basic listening skill—the skill of "checking out" what a speaker is saying. When we check out a message, we summarize what we think we've heard and give the speaker an opportunity to confirm the accuracy of our understanding. If it's inaccurate, they have the opportunity to correct any distortions in the message. Here's an example of "checking out" a statement:

Mark: "I feel frustrated when you leave the newspapers in different rooms of the house, and I have to search all over to find them. I'd like you to be considerate of my needs."

Betty: "I need to check out what I'm hearing you say. I hear you say that you're upset because I don't put the newspapers in one place. You want me to be considerate of your needs and set them in the same place every day. Is that what you said?"

Mark: "That's right."

By "checking out" what Mark said, Betty has learned that she accurately heard Mark's message. How does she know this? Mark has told her. This process is useful because it is easy for listeners to misinterpret what a speaker says.

The Problem of Meaning

One of the reasons for "checking out" what the speaker has said is that words mean different things to different people in different contexts. I recall seeing a cartoon of a customer standing in front of a pharmacy counter. He was reading a sign that said, "We dispense with accuracy." What a confusing message! It might mean that the pharmacist took great pains to be accurate. Or it might mean the opposite: "We don't try to be accurate." I'd want to check out what they meant before I let them fill my prescription!

• Communicating is a process of sending and receiving meanings. •

The cartoonist played off our tendency to use words that have double or triple interpretations. The cartoon points to a basic problem. Communicating is a process of sending and receiving *meanings*. And since words can mean different things at different times to different people, there is a great potential for confusion.

Now let's add another problem to the issue. *Meanings are in people, not in words.* The majority of people assume the opposite. They believe that meanings are in words. Just pull the dictionary off the shelf and look up the meaning. That won't work with most words that we use in daily conversations. Let me illustrate.

Imagine that I have an eighteen-year-old son. I say to him, "Son, I don't want you to be out late tonight." He replies, "Don't worry, Dad. I've got an exam at school tomorrow, and I won't be out late. I want to be in early tonight."

•

Meanings are in people, not in words.

•

What did I mean by "late"? 10:00 P.M.? 11:45 P.M.? 2:00 A.M.? And what did my son mean by "early"? 9:30 P.M.? 11:00 P.M.? 2:00 A.M.? If "early" to him was 11:45 P.M. and to me it was more like 10:00 P.M., we are liable to get into an argument.

This leads us to still another problem related to meanings. *Much of our communication deals with abstract ideas.* Whenever we communicate in the abstract, we are likely to be misunderstood. Most of us don't realize how often we talk about theoretical or conceptual matters. Words like love, happiness, morality, good, valuable, and faithful are relative to the speaker's and listener's reference points.

I'm reminded of last year's political elections. Much of the rhetoric the candidates used concerned "family values." What I found fascinating was that individuals were espousing values that could be interpreted as destructive to the traditional family, but they vehemently defended them as "family values." Their reference point was significantly different, yet the same language was being used.

Unless we link abstract words with specific, concrete objects, behaviors, or situations, we will consistently have communication breakdown. You may mean one thing, but your message might be misinterpreted. And remember, *the higher the level of abstraction, the greater is the potential for confusion in meaning.*

I have a clipping from our local newspaper. The author was discussing information a student brought home from his high school. The story read as follows: "Our school's cross-graded, multi-ethnic, individualized learning program is designed to enhance the concept of an open-ended learning program with emphasis on a continuum of multi-ethnic, academically enriched learning using the identified intellectually gifted child as the agent or director of his own learning. Major emphasis is on cross-graded, multi-ethnic learning with the main objective being to learn respect for the uniqueness of a person."

> •
>
> The higher the level
> of abstraction,
> the greater
> is the potential
> for confusion
> in meaning.
>
> •

You may find it hard to believe someone would write in such a complex fashion. But after more than thirty years of marriage, parenting five children to adulthood, and working with people for years in all sorts of situations, I know that this happens frequently. And I know how easy it is to get into relational difficulties because we were using the same words, but thinking different thoughts. We consistently assume that we know what the other person means when frequently we don't. Trouble follows!

By using the shared-meaning process, the listener can check out the meaning of the speaker's words, and more accurate communication will take place.

The Problem of Perception

Another problem that "checking out" solves is the matter of *perception*. Consider the following facts:

1. Perception is a personal process. Each person sees, hears, and processes words through his or her own unique grid. For example, someone may use the

125

word "black" to refer to evil. Another person may take offense at this and see the comment as racist.
2. Perception is a discriminating process. Each person selects information that he decides is important and omits what to him is unimportant. Another person may look at the same situation and value as important what the first person rejected. This happens all the time in marital relationships. The wife may value words of love, but her husband may see them as unnecessary.
3. Perception is an experience-based process. We interpret information and situations through the grid of our life experiences. Each person brings his unique set of experiences. The word "submissive" may mean inferior or second rate to a woman who has been demeaned by men.
4. Perception is an interpretive process. My perception leads me to read meaning, value, purpose, motive, and so on into life situations. This is inevitable because we all have a need to find purpose and meaning in life.

I have been fascinated by how two scholars interpret the same biblical passage in different ways. Their theological frame of reference prompts them to see different meanings in the same event. You may not be a seminary professor, but I'm sure you recognize how you see situations differently than others around you.

Perception, then, becomes an inescapable reality in communication. I listen to others in a way that will make sense of what is being said. And the way that it will make sense to me is by the way I perceive it. Hopefully, after I have processed the information, I will run it by the speaker to make sure the message matches my understanding.

The Problems of Assumptions and Distortions

Listeners often assume they already know what the speaker is going to say or what it means. Once, as a graduate student, I sat in a conference room listening to a fellow student's presentation. He asked another student, "Do you know what I mean?" and the other student replied, "Yes, I know *exactly* what you mean." I remember wondering, "Does he really know *exactly* what the speaker means?"

The popular game of "Rumor" further illustrates the possibilities for faulty communication. In this fun activity, one person whispers a message to the person next to him, who whispers it to the third person, and so on around the room until the message returns to the one who started the game. The humor emerges in the gross distortion that usually occurs. This simple game teaches us about the nature of communication: it is easily distorted and needs "checking out" for accuracy.

Unfortunately, "checking out" is not done in most communication. A husband does not typically say, "Let me tell you what I heard you say. I want to be certain I've heard you correctly." More likely, he assumes that what he thought he heard was what his wife actually meant and doesn't realize how significantly his internal filters and faulty listening skills have changed the message. Because messages are so often distorted, they need "checking out" to ensure their accuracy.

> •
> Communication is easily distorted and needs "checking out" for accuracy.
> •

The value of "checking out" goes beyond accuracy of communication, however, as important as that is. When we practice this discipline, we are expressing a commitment to the other person. The action tells the person that we have a genuine interest in him or her. We show respect for their ideas, needs, and values. No doubt you can see that "checking out" is another tangible way to invest in a quality relationship.

Getting to a Shared Meaning

The process of reaching a shared meaning is to be used—not just studied. Therefore, I would like to outline the process as clearly as possible, so that you will understand how to implement it in your relationships.

Step 1: The Speaker Sends the Message

Message sent

Shared
Meaning
Process

In this step, the individual who is concerned about an issue and wants to reach a shared meaning goes to the other person and tells him or her: "I'd like to have a shared meaning with you." (Of course, both partners should know about the process and be able to work through it.) The speaker then describes the issue as clearly and simply as possible using a factual, self-reporting approach rather than blaming, ridiculing, or accusing the other person.

It is best for the speaker to send the message in small units interspersed with listener "check outs" as described earlier. Remember that overload of information is a common communication problem. A good rule of thumb is to speak for about twenty seconds and then ask the listener for feedback; it is probably impossible for a listener to give feedback for a longer message with any degree of accuracy. Some couples find it helpful to have a signal, such as a raised hand, whereby the listener indicates "That's all I can handle; let me check out for accuracy."

At the end of the message, the speaker invites a shared-meaning response by stating, "What have you heard me say?" This statement leads to the second step.

Step 2: The Listener Reports Back

Next, the listener describes as precisely as possible what he has heard the speaker say. His or her goal is to match the speaker's message accurately. The listener will probably paraphrase the information but must avoid adding his or her own opinion, interpretation, or meaning to the speaker's message. There is no place in the shared meaning process for statements like these:

"You said you love me, but I don't think you mean it."
"I heard you say you want to be more helpful with household chores—but you just said that because you feel guilty about my being overworked."

Think about it. Isn't it frustrating to speak to someone, wanting to be understood, only to have her or him change the intent of what you are saying? Doesn't such behavior tend to stifle one's communication? In the shared-meaning process, the listener's response should be devoid of counsel, admonition, criticism, or commentary; it should be a simple and accurate report of what he or she heard.

When the listener finishes reporting back, he or she says, "Is that what you said? Is that what you meant?" This statement in turn leads to step 3.

Step 3: The Speaker Acknowledges the Listener's Accuracy

At this point, the speaker has two courses of action. If he is satisfied that the listener has heard him accurately, he can respond by saying, "Yes, that's what I said." Or if he feels that the listener has misunderstood, omitted, or distorted his message, he can clarify what the listener missed and request another response by again asking, "What did you hear me say?"

The shared-meaning process can be as simple as the three steps I've outlined above, or it can go on with more speaker-listener exchanges until the participants are satisfied that the message has been sent and received.

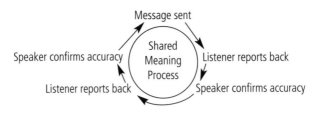

130

Occasionally someone will express frustration that the phrases "I hear you say" and "Are you saying?" sound canned or artificial. Whenever we are learning a new skill, it feels awkward and unnatural. (Remember when you learned to drive a car?) If you are willing to be patient with yourself and others who are trying to master this skill, you'll become more comfortable and relaxed. You'll find the words that convey the concept in your language. Just don't let the awkwardness keep you from mastering this valuable communication tool.

You may be asking, "How much time does this process take?" It could be as brief as saying, "I'm not certain what you mean by 'Your words hurt me.' Could you clarify what I said that hurt?" Or it could be a process that takes ten to fifteen minutes because the missed meaning represents a deeper issue. My concern is that you understand the need to clarify meanings and that you learn the process to do that.

Another question people ask is "Can it be used with someone who hasn't read the book or who doesn't understand the concept?" My experience is that when I adopt positive, effective communication principles, the odds are in my favor that the other person will respond positively. Proverbs 15:1 says, "A gentle answer turns away wrath, but a harsh word stirs up anger." If I practice speaking in a soft, gentle, and compassionate tone, the other person usually will settle down and interact with me in a healthier manner. In the same way, when I genuinely want to know what another person means by a statement, they will likely realize that I care about our relationship and don't want to presume that I know everything.

Shared meaning means mutual understanding, but it does not necessarily imply agreement. My wife may say to me, "Norm, I understand that you want to take five thousand dollars out of the bank to buy a motorcycle. I don't think that's a good use for the money. Besides, you're getting too old to be riding a motorcycle!" It is unrealistic to think that two people will, or should, agree on everything. But we all want to be understood and to have our feelings respected. The goal of this chapter is to explore the process of arriving at mutual understanding.

•
Shared meaning
means mutual
understanding,
but it does
not necessarily
imply agreement.
•

Through the consistent application of the process, many relational struggles can be reduced, and many communication distortions can be straightened out. People who learn to reach a shared meaning will have better feelings about their relationships because they will have achieved greater mutual understanding. Gaining a shared meaning is more apt to build friendships than feuds.

(• Time to Reflect and Apply

Since this information is probably new to you, it will take more than reading this chapter to make the shared-meaning concept usable. What you are learning you must begin to apply. This involves three essential steps: practice, practice, and practice! The exercises that follow will help you gain a better feeling for the shared-meaning process. Work through each step with a partner.

1. Checking Up on Yourself

The following statements will help you evaluate your understanding and need for the shared-meaning process.

1.	I recognize that others hold different ideas, values, and perceptions than I do.	Never	Sometimes	Usually
2.	I help others clarify my meanings by asking, "What did you hear me say?"	Never	Sometimes	Usually
3.	I check out other people's meanings with statements like "What I hear you saying is _____ "	Never	Sometimes	Usually
4.	When misunderstandings occur, I am vulnerable to making accusations or ridiculing.	Never	Sometimes	Usually

2. Weekly Journaling

This week write down your thoughts concerning the following issues:

- In what situations do you often feel misunderstood?
- Who seems to often misunderstand you?
- What information in the chapter do you most need to apply?

3. Going Further

The following exercises will help you understand and apply the information from this chapter.

1. List several issues you would like to discuss with someone and the specific persons with whom you would like to discuss these issues. The issues should be ones where you desire to reach a shared meaning.

Person   Issue

_____   _____

_____   _____

_____   _____

Person	Issue
_____	_____
_____	_____
_____	_____
_____	_____
_____	_____
_____	_____
_____	_____

Do the persons involved understand the shared-meaning concept? If not, how could you acquaint them with it?

2. Schedule time with the persons you have listed above. Remember to plan time when both of you are rested, relaxed, and undistracted. Work through the shared-meaning process.
3. Evaluate the outcome of your discussion:
   a. Did you follow the three-step process?
   b. Did you stay on the issue?
   c. Did you avoid accusations, ridicule, and name-calling?
   d. Did you understand your partner's communication?
   e. Did your partner understand yours?
4. Extra practice: Role-play the following situations using the shared-meaning process. Take turns being the sender and receiver.
   a. Your partner has not been keeping the bankbook balanced.
   b. You and your partner differ on child-rearing practices. Each holds out for his or her way.
   c. Your partner has left you at home too many nights. You feel lonely and neglected.
   d. Your parents are coming to visit. They are critical of you and your spouse.

e. Your relationship with your partner is unsatis-fying.
f. You and your partner plan to purchase a new automobile. You have different preferences.
g. You are starting a new job. You feel nervous and unsure of your skills.

CHAPTER EIGHT

[Personal Growth through Listening]

•

Lord, teach me to listen. The times are noisy and my ears are weary with the thousand raucous sounds that continuously assault them. Give me the spirit of the boy Samuel when he said to Thee, "Speak, for thy servant heareth." Let me hear Thy Voice, that its tones may be familiar when the sounds of earth die away and the only sound will be the music of Thy speaking Voice. Amen.[1]

A. W. Tozer

Listen to advice and accept instruction, and in the end you will be wise.

Proverbs 19:20

Visit a doctor for your annual checkup, and he'll likely use a stethoscope. This instrument allows the physician to "hear" internal noises like your heartbeat, air movement in the lungs, or sounds in the intestines. He'll listen to see if you are healthy in those hidden parts that cannot be observed by the human eye. When he looks puzzled or says, "Oh my, what do we have here?" you'll probably get nervous and think that he's found something wrong.

But you don't need a stethoscope to conduct another type of personal examination. By developing your perceptive listening skills, you can learn to listen to your mental, emotional, and spiritual health. Most of this book has focused on listening as a way to understand or assist others. In this chapter we want to refocus and consider how we can use perceptive listening skills to stimulate personal growth.

Listening is one of the primary means we have for learning about ourselves. As children, we develop our perceptions of who we are and what we are destined to become largely according to what our parents say about us: "I like you," "You're a helpful child," "You're such a crybaby." As we grow older, other voices add to those perceptions, complementing or challenging what our parents have said. By the time we reach adulthood, we have heard a myriad of voices that define, refine, or undermine who we believe we are.

Over time we filter out what we do not want to hear, modify what is incongruent with our self-perception, and absorb data that seems useful. This is called discerning listening. It is defined as the power to distinguish and select what is true or appropriate or genuinely excellent.

When we listen with discernment—to God, to other people, even to our inner selves—we grow. We gain wisdom. We mature. We discover valuable truths that help us move toward wholeness. We come to see our strengths and the areas in which we need to change. Discerning listening has the potential to move us toward the fullness of what God intended for our lives. In fact, I am so emphatic as to say that no one ever becomes Christlike without cultivating a listening heart.

Our God is not silent. He speaks. This is powerfully stated in the words of John 1:1: "In the beginning was the Word, and the Word was with God, and the Word was God." Our heavenly Father spoke clearly, powerfully, and intimately through Jesus Christ. Even now he voices his personal testimony of his nature through his Holy Spirit. He expresses his profound concern for each of us. He says, "I love you."

A. W. Tozer underscored this truth when he wrote, "The facts are that God is not silent, has never been silent. It is the nature of God to speak. The second Person of the Holy Trinity is called the *Word*."[2] He speaks not only that we might know him, but that we might clearly understand ourselves and our relationships to him. His Spirit speaks to us through his "love letter"— the Bible—so that our lives may come into intimate relationship with him. As the intimacy deepens, we move to higher and higher levels of maturity.

God invites us to listen to him. In fact, he challenges us to listen to him. It gives him no pleasure when we live in ignorance of his remarkable plan for our lives. Our Lord doesn't want his children to live like dumb sheep. Jesus said, "He who has ears, let him hear" (Matt. 11:15). Unfortunately, we don't always heed his invitation. Isaiah grieved over Israel's refusal to hear God's voice urging them to repentance and personal growth. Jeremiah and Ezekiel joined him in expressing God's concern that his people would not listen (Isa. 6:9; Jer. 5:21; Ezek. 12:2). Jesus applied the same truth to the Jews of his day. He longed to share with them, but like stubborn children, they plugged their ears and adamantly refused to hear his voice (Mark 8:18).

We can profit from their error; we can heed the counsel of Scripture to acknowledge this ever-present danger of ignoring God's voice. We can be alert to the fact that the noise of self-interest, distractions, and daily activities can muffle the Father's counsel and instruction.

> •
> Our Lord doesn't want his children to live like dumb sheep.
> •

The fact that our all-knowing and majestic Lord speaks raises several important questions: How do we listen to God? Can we learn to know when he is speaking? How does he express himself?

God Speaks through Scripture

We are told that our Father has spoken and continues to speak through the Scriptures. They are the fundamental source he has chosen to communicate eternal life principles to his children. The Scriptures contain the words of life. Jesus said, "The words I have spoken to you are spirit and they are life" (John 6:63). When Christ's words penetrate our mind, emotions, and spirit, they have the potential to bring about genuine transformation.

The sequence of the process is: (1) he speaks, (2) I listen, (3) I believe, (4) I apply, and (5) I am changed (see John 5:24; 15:3). The essential dynamics of transformation are embodied in this process, which brings a cleansing from defeat patterns and growth in the intimate relationship to our heavenly Father (John 15:3; 17:17).

So if the Bible is the primary channel our Lord uses to speak to us, then we need to be keen to listen to him there. If we are convinced that he seeks an intimate relationship as a way to interact with us, we will set aside time to meet him in a listening, meditative spirit.

Many Christians are defeated because they view Bible reading as a duty rather than an opportunity; it becomes a chore rather than a joy, a burden rather than a delight. Maintaining a healthy mental attitude is crucial to listening to Scripture in a life-changing manner.

One day, while I was teaching in seminary, a student came to my office. He served on the pastoral staff of a local church. He had already received a graduate degree from the seminary, but had returned to take courses in Creative Bible Teaching to enrich his ministry. After he settled into his chair, he unloaded his problem.

> •
> Maintaining a healthy mental attitude is crucial to listening to Scripture in a life-changing manner.
> •

"Norm, personal Bible study is a constant struggle for me. I'll be honest with you—I don't enjoy it. When I try to do it, I get turned off. I can prepare sermons and teach Bible classes, but when it comes to studying the Bible for personal growth, I am defeated. Can you help me?"

As the conversation unfolded, I discovered that my friend had come to see the Bible as a textbook that he needed to master to pass college and seminary exams. Term papers that analyzed context, translations, and so on had clouded the personal message from a compassionate God. Bit by bit, the Lord's love letter had lost its delight.

That morning we mapped out a strategy for Bible study. My friend would spend time away from his office with a modern translation and try to rediscover a personal, relational approach to the Scripture. In the weeks that followed, he learned again how to sit in the presence of his Lord and enter into an intimate dialogue with him. Thankfully he rediscovered a lost passion and began to relish those precious encounters with his God.

Listening to the Holy Spirit

Though the Bible is a primary means by which God speaks to us, it is not the only source. Tozer notes, "The Bible is the written word of God, and because it is written it is confined and limited by the necessities of ink and paper and leather. The Voice of God, however, is alive and free as the sovereign God is free."[3]

This brings us to a second way that God speaks to us—through his indwelling Spirit. The very presence of the Holy Spirit is evidence that God is seeking to commune with us—he wants an intimate relationship. Jesus made this clear in his words recorded in John 14:26: "But the Counselor, the Holy Spirit, whom the Father will send in my name, will teach you all things and will remind you of everything I have said to you." Our Father nurtures us through the counsel of the indwelling One if we listen to him. It is crucial that we learn to discern his voice; in fact it is vital to our growth.

Years ago we crammed our family belongings into a four-door Ford Falcon and a U-Haul trailer and journeyed from Portsmouth, Virginia, to Wheaton, Illinois, where I was to pursue graduate studies. We had only traveled fifty of the eight hundred miles when I knew that our little Falcon wasn't going to make it. It was a skinny runt trying to lift an Atlas load. The seriousness of our situation left me with a deep sense of anxiety, inadequacy, and helplessness. What was I to do? I could not turn back, yet the journey ahead was in jeopardy. All that night and the following day, I felt my physical, emotional, and spiritual energy leaking out of me. Finally, with the support and counsel of my father-in-law, we decided to rent a U-Haul truck instead of a trailer and made the move in two vehicles.

The next day, Sunday, we went to church. I felt exhausted. But as I sat in the church pew, the Spirit of

God ministered to me in a powerful, loving way. I sensed his presence, comfort, and support through each hymn we sang. They seemed to have been chosen specifically for me. As he encouraged me through his love and grace, I was overwhelmed and wept with gratitude.

It is my conviction that our Lord speaks to us daily through circumstances, the quiet prompting of inner voices, the Word of God, another person, pastors, teachers, and a myriad of other sources. He counsels each of us in his own unique way. Often he encourages us to take the next step that leads to new dimensions of growth. Learning to sense his presence, knowing his voice, and developing our own ability to hear him is vital to the enrichment of our lives.

Yes, we grow by listening to God. As we listen and respond positively, we are changed—changed into his likeness.

I believe that large numbers of Christians find it difficult to listen to our Lord today. We live in a society that is inundated with messages that constantly bombard us. Radios, televisions, and VCRs entice us to "tune in and tune out." An abundance of visual advertisements are posted in most public areas. In addition, more people today live with stress due to the fact that their jobs require more mental than physical energy. Is it any wonder, with this information overload, that people are too mentally weary to listen to another speaker—even if it is our Lord?

I conduct an exercise in one of my seminary classes to illustrate this phenomenon. I assign twelve students a role they are to take. The role, described on a slip of paper, is some person or influence on an individual's life. One says, "You are the voice of this person's

> •
>
> People are too mentally weary to listen to another speaker—even if it is our Lord.
>
> •

143

favorite sports team urging him to listen to the game on the radio or TV." Another might be, "You are the voice of this person's boss pressuring him to perform at a higher level." Each role is a realistic example of some "voice" that is vying for his attention.

I ask a student to come to the front of the class and sit in a chair. The other twelve individuals come to the front and stand around the seated student. Then I instruct them to claim their portion of that person's thoughts. The room is instantly filled with voices cajoling, urging, pressuring, and demanding his attention. Inevitably, the seated person feels overwhelmed.

Once I've called a halt to the confusion, I then ask each person to read the instructions on the slip of paper, beginning with person number one. When we reach person number twelve, the slip of paper reads, "You are the voice of Jesus Christ inviting this person to come and spend time with you. Your way is never to yell or demand, to shove or control. Call the person to your side."

The student in the chair *never* hears the voice of Jesus. The last time I did this exercise, I noticed that when Frank went back to his seat his eyes seemed moist as though he was emotionally touched by the experience. Later, I asked him about his reaction. He told me that the event so paralleled his own life that it frightened him. Frank is probably more like most of us than we want to admit.

Listening to Others

Are you aware of the hidden you—those habits, mannerisms, idiosyncrasies which others see, though you do not? We all have a part of us that's known to others but hidden from ourselves. There's nothing wrong with that; the trouble comes when we need to see ourselves as others see us, but are unable to do so. Sometimes it's because others are afraid to tell us; they think we will get angry, tell them to mind their own business, or break off the friendship. Thus we never get valuable information that could enrich us.

We all need feedback—essential information about ourselves given to us by others. Feedback enables us to monitor who we are and what we are doing.

Feedback is necessary because it complements the subjective view we have of ourselves. It supplements information we presently have. Sometimes feedback comes in the form of a performance evaluation, test results, or job evaluation. At other times, feedback comes when friends or family members share their perspective on a problem we are coping with. They tell us how they see us handling it, obstacles we have overlooked, or progress they feel is occurring.

Feedback that facilitates personal growth is usually most effective when the interpersonal relationship is strong. Warm, caring relationships foster an environment that is conducive to open, honest feedback. As we grow in loving concern for one another, we want to share insights that will enrich each other's lives. One reason many people never see the hidden part of their lives is that they avoid the kind of relationships that would reveal this to them.

> •
>
> One reason many people never see the hidden part of their lives is that they avoid the kind of relationships that would reveal this to them.
>
> •

What can others reveal to us about our hidden selves? What information can be given to us for our profit? Let me suggest three possibilities. *First, others can give us details about ourselves*. The facts may be neither good nor bad, but they are invaluable in gaining a fuller self-

145

portrait. For instance, I have five children: a son and four daughters. I have observed that my son, Joel, is action-oriented; he does not sit still long, and he becomes bored easily. By contrast, my daughter Jill is warm and affectionate; she is also more hesitant to act, waiting for others to begin. These basic bits of information about two of my children may shed light on how they cope with life situations. Sharing this information with them can be valuable for their self-growth.

Second, others can show us our strengths. I observe that many of us hesitate to trust our own subjective evaluations of ourselves; for example, we hesitate to declare enthusiastically, "I am a gifted teacher. I feel very happy about it." But others can point out factual data that affirms our own perception of the skills, talents, or gifts we possess. Such feedback reinforces our growing awareness of our inner potential.

> •
> Most people are helped significantly in their personal growth when we affirm the valid strengths we see in them.
> •

This point must be underscored for both speaker and listener. Most people are helped significantly in their personal growth when we affirm the valid strengths we see in them. Ephesians 4:29 states, "Do not let any unwholesome talk come out of your mouths, but only what is helpful for building others up . . . that it may benefit those who listen." Wise feedback is a powerful means of building others up by validating their strengths. One of the immense benefits of small sharing groups is the potential of encouraging and affirming positive growth in the members' lives.

One day a friend said to me, "Norm, I believe you have the gift of faith. You are a visionary. You see possibilities and opportunities others don't." Ted's thoughtful remarks were provocative. I came away from our conversation pondering what he had said. Ted's words helped me grow.

Third, others can point out areas of need and weakness in our lives—areas we have not faced. I recall hearing a denominational leader describe his encounter with a pastor who had developed a consistently negative attitude. Church members complained of his refusal to listen to new ideas and of his tendency to criticize and judge other people. Through the leader's wise and gentle feedback, this pastor came to grips with his area of need. The apostle Paul describes a similar situation in which he challenged Peter about an inconsistency in his life. He says, "When Peter came to Antioch, I opposed him to his face, because he was clearly in the wrong" (Gal. 2:11). In other words, Paul gave Peter feedback.

Consider what has been said; we listen to others to receive their perspective on our life and to see what they see. This is essential for healthy self-growth. We should carefully consider what our husband or wife says about us. We should listen thoughtfully when our children say, "Dad (or Mom), did you realize that you . . ." We should pause and reflect when a work associate points out a strength or weakness he sees. These people are helping us to see ourselves more fully.

> •
> Defensiveness can
> be a barrier
> to self-growth.
> •

Unfortunately, some people never profit from feedback. Instead, they become defensive and argue rather than listen. Such people go through life sweeping valuable information under a mental carpet, pushing it from view. They would rather keep their hidden self out of their sight than face it as a growing challenge. Some secretly know that what is being reported to them is true but outwardly deny it. Others may honestly not see the problem or opportunity before them and consistently reject sound counsel.

Defensiveness can be a barrier to self-growth. Another barrier is low self-esteem. Low self-esteem is a deadly enemy of many Christians' growth. Because they continue to believe the lie that "I am stupid," "I am incompetent," "I am ugly," and so on, they cannot believe the truth about themselves that others point out. They continue living defeated lives, accepting as truth that they are rejects, incompetent, and deficient. The positive qualities others see in them are cast aside because those qualities do not fit the image these individuals have of themselves. They do not listen to learn.

•

Low self-esteem is a deadly enemy of many Christians' growth.

•

I have not meant to imply that we should unquestioningly accept everything others say about us. If what another person says is true, he or she should be able to document it with clear facts. Then we should look at those facts honestly. In addition, we can seek the perspective of still another person who may be able to add insight or correct the first person's observations.

Look at it this way. Imagine yourself going to a physician for an examination. After the checkup he reports, "You have leukemia." Your mind reels; it seems impossible. You ask for facts—"How do you know I have this hateful disease?" He gives the results of two highly accurate tests he has administered.

You face a choice—accept the facts and begin the necessary treatment or deny the facts and continue to die. You may seek another medical opinion, but if the second doctor agrees with the first, you will again be called to face the situation and to change your life accordingly.

Throughout life we have the opportunity to listen and learn about ourselves. Feedback from others is vital for personal growth. What we do with that information may be even more strategic.

Listening to Ourselves

I cannot underscore enough the significant value of quiet, reflective times when we can get in touch with the movements of our lives. These are the times when we listen to ourselves—to the inner voice that is often drowned out in the bustle of everyday life. These occasions may lead to a reappraisal of our lifestyle, an inventory of our activities, or a commitment to face a challenge.

As we take private time to think, pray, or plan, we may discover many things. Often, when we take time to listen to our inner voice, we find an internal process that has been under way for some time. We may get in touch with *visions* we have carried for years—unfulfilled dreams that could enrich, even revolutionize, our lives. These challenges might be as incredible as sailing across the Atlantic in a ten-foot sailboat or as life changing as returning to college to study a new field that intrigues us.

Sometimes we come in touch with a *complaint* we have not faced. We may realize that our marriage is deteriorating through neglect. Perhaps an intense work schedule has choked off meaningful time spent with our partner. We may hear a voice calling us to reevaluate our priorities and to take action.

•

Most of us have no plan for quiet spaces in our lives.

•

The inner voice may point out a *pattern of life* that needs to be altered through God's power. Perhaps we've developed the habit of shutting other people out of our lives because we fear involvement. We may ponder, "Is it too late for me to change? Could I face the fear and discover the joy of relationships?"

Listening to ourselves—to the inner voice—involves making two decisions. The first decision is to seek out moments of silence. This practice is not common to our culture. Most of us have no plan for quiet spaces in our lives. *We must deliberately choose to seek out silence and plan it into our daily activities.*

I believe that it is healthy for each Christian to budget time daily for a minimum of fifteen minutes of personal reflection and meditation. During that time, we should try to sense the issues and concerns that we are grappling with internally. We should try to focus on them as clearly as possible and sense what we are being called to do.

I must stress the importance of silence. This may appear obvious, but it is crucial; to listen to our inner selves, we must find a place as quiet as possible. It may be helpful to keep a diary or journal of insights and thoughts that come to mind.

The second decision necessary for listening to our inner selves is the decision to act. Personal growth is typically an act of faith. It requires a step in a new direction, opening a new chapter in our lives, attempting something we have never tried before, and conquering a hurdle that seems impossibly high. As we interact with God about these inner concerns, we will inevitably be led to a faith decision. I was discussing this chapter with a friend, and she pointed out the cyclic nature of the process. The diagram below illustrates the cycle:

Through times of meditative silence, we become self-aware. As we become self-aware and interact with the Spirit of God, we are inevitably brought to a decision point. Will we act? Will we draw upon God's resources and our own resources to act upon this new challenge before us? Dialogue with the indwelling Spirit will engender motivation. As we act in faith, pursuing the challenge, we grow. However, the process does not end here. The newfound growth leads to new insight, which is fed into new times of meditative silence, which leads to greater self-awareness, and so on.

Thus we can see the potential for three dynamic processes operating in our lives. As we become skilled listeners, we hear the voice of God—guiding, teaching, enriching, and affirming us. We hear the voices of other people providing invaluable input for our growth processes. Finally, we recognize an internal voice of the self, making us aware of important life issues we can tackle. These three processes, when functioning healthily, provide incredible potential to stretch, nurture, enrich—yes, even revolutionize—our lives.

Time to Reflect and Apply

Personal growth comes through the application of truths we discover. Thus it is important for us to respond to what we are learning. The following exercises will guide you in that process.

1. Checking Up on Yourself

Take time now to reflect on your own growth process by circling your response to each statement below.

151

1. I listen to God through the reading of the Scriptures.	Never	Sometimes	Usually
2. I listen for God through the circumstances he arranges in my life.	Never	Sometimes	Usually
3. I listen for God in the insights of discerning Christians.	Never	Sometimes	Usually
4. I seek feedback from others to better understand my strengths.	Never	Sometimes	Usually
5. I seek feedback from others to better understand my weaknesses.	Never	Sometimes	Usually
6. I keep a diary or journal to keep track of what I am learning about myself.	Never	Sometimes	Usually
7. I have regular times of quietness for reflection and solitude.	Never	Sometimes	Usually

2. Weekly Journaling

Write out your thoughts during the week about the following issues:

- Jot down facts or feelings about your personal growth that you are aware of.
- Where do you desire growth in your life? What is hindering that growth?
- What friend could support you and hold you accountable as you take steps toward maturity?

3. Going Further

Work through the following exercises to continue to process the ideas in this chapter.

1. Earlier I asked, "How do we listen to God?" I'd like you to respond to that personally. Jot down several ways that you typically listen to God. Then reflect on what you have read in this chapter. Have other ways been suggested? If so, add them to your list and consider how to put them into practice.

2. Helping others grow is as important as your own growth. The chart below will help you think through strengths you see in your family members and friends. Plan specific ways to affirm their strengths (note in mail, phone call, personal visit, etc.).

Person	Strength
_____	_____
_____	_____
_____	_____
_____	_____
_____	_____
_____	_____

3. Complete the following statement: The time and place I will reserve for personal meditation is

_____

_____.

CHAPTER NINE

[Becoming a Powerful, Perceptive Listener]

•

If I could stand for five minutes at His vantage point and see the entire scheme of things as He sees it, how absurd would be my dreads, how ridiculous my fears and tears![1]

Vance Havner

But solid food is for the mature, who because of practice have their senses trained to discern good and evil.

Hebrews 5:14 NASB

For a quarter of a century I've been learning how to be an effective, perceptive listener. It's helped me be a better husband, father, and grandfather. It has enriched my compassion for others and allowed me to mirror the tender heart of our Lord. It has made me wiser.

I began to taste the fruit of this quest several years after I started to grow as a listener. Our family was on a long weekend campout with Winnie's brother and sister-in-law and their two children. We were seated around a blazing campfire sharing what we appreciated about each other. It was an intimate, affirming time.

My oldest daughter, Amy, spoke.

"Dad, one thing I appreciate about you is that you're a good listener. When I want to talk, I know that you'll pay attention to what I say. It means a lot to know you care enough to listen."

Wow! A warm, enjoyable feeling swept over me. I felt encouraged hearing that my commitment to be a better listener was meaningful to my daughter. My effort was bearing fruit.

Perhaps you're thinking, "Norm's ready to claim the good listener award! I hope it doesn't go to his head." But to be honest with you, I recognize that becoming a truly skillful perceptive listener is a lifelong process. I feel as challenged today to continue monitoring my attitudes and skills toward listening as I did when I first caught the vision. I know myself! If I'm not diligent, I can become careless and insensitive to the messages others are sending me. I don't want that to happen.

> •
>
> Becoming a truly skillful perceptive listener is a lifelong growth process.
>
> •

For the past two days, Winnie and I have had two supercharged grandchildren, Ben and Jane, staying with us. Laughter, screams, chatter, and other "noises" have invaded our quiet, intimate house. Last night I was tired and thinking, "Tomorrow they go home!" But immediately I was aware of another voice. It reminded me that if I took time to become involved with them, I could communicate the genuine love I felt for them. So I helped Ben shampoo and rinse his hair, and I played Go Fish with Jane. When they went to bed, I was gratified that I had taken time to be with them and communicate my interest in them. Someday when they are older, they may need a listening ear, and I want them to know I'm available.

Perceptive listening is a combination of healthy attitudes and well-honed skills. This entire book has been my attempt to address both dimensions. However, *perceptive listening is rooted in a series of skills that a person continually practices, honing them until they become a natural part of life*. You may have read the earlier chapters and gained valuable information from them. But the only way to grow as a listener is to practice the essential listening skills. In this chapter I identify six basic skills you can practice, polish, and perfect.

The Power of Observation

The first skill involves strengthening our power of observation. It includes what I discern before, during, and after a person speaks. The skill of observation is listening with your eyes. How skilled are you at noticing a person who is discouraged, lonely, upset, or joyous? What facial cues do you look for? Do you observe the tired look, the slouched back, or the discouraged tone of voice in another?

•

The skill of observation is listening with your eyes.

•

If a couple came to your home for supper, would you be able to spot a coolness in their relationship that might indicate they had just had an argument? When listening to a friend on the telephone, could you hear the discouragement, loneliness, or anger in his or her voice? While waiting in the checkout line, could you detect the irritation the cashier was feeling toward a shopper? As you stand before your class, can you feel the joy in one student's voice and the sorrow in another's?

Think of the following situations. How does what you observe prepare you for perceptive listening?

- Your child comes home from school, slams the door, and stomps into her bedroom.
- An employee is seated in your office. He keeps looking down and rubs his hands on his knees.
- In the Bible class you teach, Mrs. Gomez looks nervously at her husband when you talk about tithing, and he shrugs his shoulders.
- Shoshana is telling you that her boyfriend broke up with her last night. You notice that there is moisture around her eyes.

In each situation, individuals are exhibiting behaviors that give us clues about what they might be thinking or feeling. You can increase your observational skills by learning to ask yourself the following questions.

What behavior is this person exhibiting that seems unusual or out of place? Imagine that you have a friend who is typically outgoing and cheerful. One day you stop by her house to visit and she seems moody and non-communicative. You leave feeling puzzled, but don't express what you have observed. If you had, she might have unburdened the pain she was feeling from a hurtful situation that occurred earlier in the day. Her husband had criticized her unjustly, leaving her feeling despondent and defeated. She really did need someone to listen. The clues were there, but you were in a rush to get home. You lost an opportunity to help a person in need.

Even physical distance could be an indication that the person is acting in a peculiar manner. Or the way he or she is dressed. Or the lack of personal grooming. All are behavioral cues that something is out of order in the person's life.

What emotions appear to be present in the person's life? I have mentioned earlier that many people do not identify their emotional states with specific emotional words. More frequently they act out their feelings.

- The angry person speaks in a sharp tone of voice.
- The discouraged person speaks softly while gazing at the floor.
- The ecstatic person dances around the room with a broad grin on his face.
- The grieving person suddenly weeps.

Some emotional outbursts are strongly related to a specific emotion. Others are less definite. But the person who has trained his powers of observation will detect the presence of some emotion. He then feeds back his observation to the other person to see if this might open up a conversation in which the person can process the underlying emotion.

Recently my daughter Annette was met by her sister Amy at Denver International Airport. Annette had been on vacation visiting some of her friends here in Phoenix. When she came down the jet way, Amy noticed that her sister's lip quivered. Amy commented to her sister that she looked like she was about to cry. Annette sat down and began to weep. Amy's alertness to an emotional cue opened up a conversation about Annette's vacation and the emotions she had experienced.

Does the person's communication seem awkward, uncomfortable, or out of character? Learn to notice both verbal and nonverbal characteristics of how people typically speak. Study their facial expressions, tone of voice, body language, and speech habits. This will help us sense when they are not following their usual manner.

The Power of the Setting

The second skill we need to hone is what I call the setting skill. Listening always takes place in some setting. What surrounds the speaker and listener? What is the environment like? What other people, objects, or activities are going on that invade your space? What interruptions, distractions, or influences are present? Too often the speaker and listener do not take into account the setting in which their communication occurs. The setting can make the difference between a productive and a painful exchange.

I remember a time when Winnie and I were visiting relatives. It was late at night and we were in bed. I had no thoughts about pillow conversation. I am not a "night person," so when my head hits the pillow, my shades go down and I'm thinking about sleep. But unknown to me, Winnie had experienced a painful discussion with a family member and needed a listening ear. When she began to express her hurt, I was unprepared and didn't respond with empathy or compassion.

Perhaps you've guessed the outcome!

Because it was a poor setting—I was physically and mentally tired—we did not connect. As I look back on the situation, I realize that it would have helped if I had known about the encounter earlier and mentally prepared myself to be attentive.

Learn to take charge of *distractions*. I recall a time when I was at a retreat center, and a participant wanted to talk with me about a personal problem. As we seated ourselves, I was immediately aware that I was facing a wide window. People were intermittently passing by. I knew I would be constantly distracted, and so I rearranged our chairs so both of us were facing away from the window. My ability to concentrate on the speaker increased by at least 50 percent.

•

The skillful listener will consciously take charge of distracting circumstances.

•

I see many situations in which individuals do not consciously look at the room arrangement to remove distractions that will inhibit perceptive listening. The distance that people sit from each other, a room that is too warm, lights that are too bright, music or voices in an adjoining room will make focusing difficult for many individuals. The skillful listener will consciously take charge of distracting circumstances.

Remember, what may not bother you may disturb another person's concentration. Create the setting that is best for *both the speaker and the listener*. The setting may determine the outcome of your conversation. If a husband and wife try to work through a problem while children run through the house or the television is on, both may end up frustrated, discouraged, and defeated.

•

Create the setting that is best for both the speaker and the listener.

•

Also, become skilled at *monitoring each person's physical state*. Certain physical conditions reduce the potential for perceptive listening. Years ago, I was teaching at a seminary in southern California. I had a twenty- to thirty-minute commute home. When I arrived home, five young children and a wife greeted me at the door. The children were bubbling over, eager to tell me about their day's activities. Most times I had ample physical, mental, and emotional reserves to listen with genuine interest.

But not always.

Sometimes my day had been especially wearying—a heavy teaching load, a trying committee meeting, traffic jams. When I opened the door and was greeted by all those smiling faces, dancing eyes, and eager voices, I wanted to hide! But instead I learned to ask for fifteen minutes to stretch out on the bed and "unwind." In that brief time this husband and dad was getting ready to involve himself in his family members' lives.

Sometimes it's emotional limitations that create a poor setting for listening to occur. If you are emotionally stressed, you will probably find it difficult to listen. It may be better to acknowledge your emotional overload. Ask for a "time-out" to take a walk around the block, pray, and settle down. Let the person know that you want to listen, but need the opportunity to gain a better emotional state. Help the person to see that it is for his or her benefit.

The Power of Perspective Taking

The third skill is the ability to take another person's perspective: to think, feel, and see what that person is thinking, feeling, and seeing. Perspective taking moves our focus from ourselves to the other person. Obviously we can't literally get inside that person's skin, but we can hone the skill of consciously looking at life through the other person's eyes.

Once in a graduate studies class, I gave students the following assignment: "Here is a list of words Christians commonly use. Your task is to find out what fourth through sixth grade children know about these words."

One word was "trinity." The next time we met together, Jason was eager to tell me of his experience.

"Prof, this was a fascinating assignment. Let me tell you what I discovered.

"David said the word trinity meant to go on and on and on. Danny thought it meant always. They had confused it with the word eternity. I was interested in the identification they made with a similar sound. Later when I asked them what 'tri' meant, Tim volunteered, three. I then asked what three it might refer to. Tim said, 'The three that died on the cross. You know, Jesus and the two men, one on each side.' Danny thought it referred to the Father, Jesus, and the Holy Spirit. He said it so quietly that the other boys didn't hear him speak."

Then Jason added a surprise twist to the account. He said that the following evening he was visiting with the Sunday school department leader for the age group he'd interviewed. During the conversation Jason told him about his discussion with the students. When he finished the leader looked shocked. He said, "We just finished a study of the trinity with the children!"

How unfortunate that the children's teacher hadn't taken time to ask the students about their understanding of the trinity and then listened silently to grasp their perspective. If their understanding—their point of view—had been sought, the teacher's effectiveness would have increased remarkably.

We all have our own frame of reference from which we understand life and interpret circumstances. By reflecting on what a speaker's life is like, we gain insight into why he reacts and speaks as he does. Consider the following situations:

- What is it like to be a single parent who works all day and has to come home to meal preparation, children's homework, washing, and ironing? In addition, he or she is lonely for friendship with someone of the opposite sex.

- What is it like to be a teen who is failing algebra and believes that his teacher doesn't like him? When he goes home, his dad tells him he's too tired to help with his homework. "You'll just have to try harder," he says. But working harder doesn't change anything. He can't seem to think in algebraic terms.
- What is it like to be an outwardly successful businessman who inwardly feels like a failure? He knows how to make money, but has little sense of fulfillment or accomplishment.
- What is it like to be seventy-six years old and cooped up in a small room with someone else in a nursing home? Your spouse has died, all your personal mementos are gone and few people come to visit you.

The list could go on for several pages identifying the unique problems that make up each individual's life. While we can never fully grasp the other person's point of view, the fact that we try to understand communicates a powerful message. People want to know that we realize how life looks through their eyes.

Perspective taking is a skill we can learn. It involves at least two actions. First, I determine to learn as much as I can about the person. One of the best ways is by asking that individual to tell me about his life. I ask questions that probe how he feels and what he values. Then I listen carefully for how he understands or interprets the circumstances he has experienced.

Second, I ask myself, "What is it like . . . ?" completing the sentence with the facets of that individual's life.

In doing that I frequently get in touch with something I might otherwise overlook.

I experienced that when my father-in-law was in his mid-eighties. He had always had an active life, giving himself to others and the cause of Christ. He had been a bright, alert, cheerful man. He served in responsible places of Christian leadership. Others looked to him for help.

But when Wil began to experience memory loss, with increasing confusion and distortion, he became unsure of himself. He became dependent on others for supervision.

I had to ask myself, "What does life look like to Wil? What do I need to see through his eyes? What do I need to feel that Wil is feeling?"

The perspective-taking skill is valuable in building and maintaining interpersonal relationships. This skill teaches us that *things may not be as they appear to us.* It makes us cautious about making judgments and decisions without hearing from others.

> •
> The perspective-taking skill is valuable in building and maintaining interpersonal relationships.
> •

The story is told of a demanding employer who observed a man standing outside his plant smoking a cigarette. Upset with his idleness, he asked, "How much are you being paid?" "Eight-fifty an hour," was the reply. The owner handed him eighty dollars and said, "Get out and don't come back!" A few minutes later, the foreman came out and asked, "Where's that delivery man who was waiting for me?"

The owner's wrong perspective cost him eighty dollars!

The Power of Listening for Feelings

To be a truly perceptive listener, we need to sharpen a fourth skill: the ability to identify and empathize with

165

others' feelings. If you do this well, others will perceive that you care about them. They will know that you are not merely hearing them out, but listening between the words for the real message of the heart.

You must respect the emotions underlying what is being said. Otherwise, when a child says, "My teacher doesn't like me," we might respond with, "That's a foolish thing to say. Of course she likes you," or, "Well, if you'd pay more attention she'd probably like you better." The wise parent explores the child's remarks and tries to understand the emotions.

In chapter 4 we discussed listening for emotions in greater detail, but let me summarize the fundamental skills. They are:

- learning what the basic emotions are
- developing skill in identifying potential emotions through nonverbal clues
- listening for emotional content in the message
- asking for clarification of what you are sensing

The perceptive listener who is skillful in helping people talk out their emotions will be valued.

The Power of a Wise Response

One of the most common mistakes ineffective listeners make is inappropriate responses to the speaker's message. They have not developed the fifth skill: the skill of making the wise, appropriate response. Perceptive listening is rooted in patience that lets another speak freely, discernment to understand the message behind the words, and wisdom to know when and how to respond. Each skill moves us to a higher level of competency.

The starting point is to wait a moment before responding to the speaker. The counsel of James is rightly focused: "Everyone should be quick to listen, *slow to speak* and slow to become angry" (James 1:19, italics mine). This is a difficult skill for most of us to learn. We have an instinctive urge to say something to fill silent spaces. The effective listener gives the speaker ample time to communicate fully. In fact, the effective listener invites the speaker to share freely. Shakespeare said it succinctly, "Give every man thy ear, but few thy voice."

A second dimension of the response skill involves learning to *respond* rather than *react*. Remember that the primary goal of listening is to understand, to discern, and to empathize. A reacting response tends to take issue with what has been said. It is more likely to lead to a debate or argument. When I react, I want to correct what you have said. When I respond, I want to gain a better understanding.

> •
>
> Remember that the primary goal of listening is to understand, to discern, and to empathize.
>
> •

A response has a different focus. It demonstrates respect for the speaker. It seeks to understand when agreement may not be possible. If I'm listening effectively, my response will invite you to clarify your meaning, identify your emotions, and give me additional insight.

This leads me to a third aspect of the skillful response. It should not be defensive. Sometimes the person talking to us expresses negative, or even hostile, emotions toward us. If I want to hear the full communication, I put aside my emotional reaction and continue to seek to understand what the speaker has to say. Though this is not always easy, it is possible.

When you allow a speaker to express his ideas, emotions, and concerns, the time comes when he will seek your perspective, want your insights, and even become open to your counsel. If, however, you respond too quickly, you short-circuit that process. The door for full communication closes and may be more difficult to open again.

Now for a fourth skill that is part of the skillful response: *paraphrasing*. In my judgment—based on many years of observing people—this is a rarely used skill. Yet it consistently pays high dividends.

What is paraphrasing? Simply saying back what the speaker has said as clearly and accurately as possible. Then waiting to see if he acknowledges that your understanding of his message was accurate. True paraphrasing contains no hidden agendas.

- I don't attack what you've said.
- I don't dispute what you've said.
- I don't interpret what you've said.
- I don't add to what you've said.

Paraphrasing gives you the opportunity to check the accuracy of your perception by saying in your words what you have heard the speaker say. This is not a complicated skill to develop. It may be as simple as saying, "Let me tell you what I heard you say to see if I've heard you correctly." Then the message is repeated back and the speaker is asked if it was accurate. (Go back and review chapter 7.)

Above All—Demonstrate That You Care

Most people think of demonstrating care as an attitude, not a skill. But while this sixth skill is rooted in our attitude of loving concern, it is also a skill that we can develop. I've found that many individuals who think they are sympathetic and compassionate are not perceived that way because they do not exhibit behavior consistent with it.

Practicing the listening skills I've outlined in this chapter should help you become a perceptive listener. I have found them to be invaluable in my relationships at home, work, church, or in the community. They are a specific way to say, "I care about you."

One way to communicate love is by giving the other person my *focused attention.* Maintaining eye contact is a simple, but remarkable way to say you are interested in what the other person is talking about. You respect that person enough to listen to their ideas, their hurts, their cries for help."

The gospel of Jesus Christ places a high value on human life. We are not machines to be manipulated or animals to be herded, driven, or bullied. Our relationships with one another are to be characterized by compassion, tenderness, empathy, and respect. As others open their lives to us and we listen carefully to gain insight into their concerns, problems, and hurts, we can come alongside to support them in a tangible way.

Perceptive listening combines the act of love to the lonely and discouraged, the gift of discernment to the confused and bewildered, and the ministry of support for those who need a loving friend. Individuals who have ears to hear can indeed love others powerfully.

Time to Reflect and Apply

This chapter helps you identify several skill areas that strengthen you as a listener. The following assessment and practice exercises will help you achieve that goal.

1. Checking Up on Yourself

Complete the following personal assessment to gain a better understanding of your strengths and weaknesses as a listener.

1. I make a conscious effort to "size up" the environment when I listen to another person.	Never	Sometimes	Usually
2. I can spot inconsistent or unusual behavior when I am listening.	Never	Sometimes	Usually
3. I am effective in observing clues to emotional states.	Never	Sometimes	Usually
4. When listening, I remove distractions.	Never	Sometimes	Usually
5. I monitor my physical, mental, and emotional readiness to listen.	Never	Sometimes	Usually
6. I consciously think through what the speaker's point of view might be.	Never	Sometimes	Usually
7. I am able to identify potential emotions that the speaker may have and check them out.	Never	Sometimes	Usually
8. I listen patiently until the speaker finishes and then make an appropriate response.	Never	Sometimes	Usually

2. Weekly Journaling

Try to be aware of your strengths and weaknesses as a listener this week, and let your journaling reflect what you have discovered.

- I was aware that I didn't listen perceptively today when _____ was speaking to me.

170

- How could I have been more discerning in that kind of situation?
- The person that I want to give me regular feedback on my listening skills is _____ .
- I'll talk to him/her about it _____ .

3. *Going Further*

A valuable exercise to end this study would be to write down two or three specific growth goals that you would like to achieve as a listener. Then set up your own schedule to achieve them. Here are some examples:

1. Within the next thirty days, I want to learn to stop interrupting Julie when she speaks to me.
2. For the next three weeks, I will monitor my relationships with my employees to become more skilled in identifying their emotions.
3. Over the next two months, I will read through the Psalms to find Scriptures that describe my Lord as a listener.

(Remember, set the goals that you know will make you stronger as a listener.)

CHAPTER TEN

[To Bore or Not to Bore]

●

Sixty years ago I knew everything; now I know nothing; education is a progressive discovery of our own
ignorance.[1]

Will Durant

The tongue of the wise commends knowledge, but the
mouth of the fool gushes folly.

Proverbs 15:2

I'm assuming that you chose to read this book because
you want to be an effective, perceptive listener. And my

goal has been to help you get there. But before we're finished, I want to challenge you to look at the flip side of the coin. Most of us want others to listen to us. So how do we create a positive environment so that others will want to do that? No doubt you can think of individuals whom you try to avoid. When you see them, you think, "Oh no, here comes Miss Boring, Mrs. Longwinded, or Mr. I. M. Stupid! Where can I hide?"

Robert Louis Stevenson said, "All speech, whether written or spoken, is in a dead language until it finds a willing and prepared hearer."[2] He reminds us that speakers need to have something worth saying if they expect us to listen. Too often they violate the most basic principles of communication and then wonder why no one listens to them. Thus learning to speak so that others will listen is a worthy goal for us to pursue.

I've never forgotten a wise statement a friend of mine said about this issue. "If we took seriously the principle that people do not listen effectively, we would change the way we teach." As one who has spent a lifetime in teaching and preaching settings, I appreciate the wisdom of my friend's words. I am probably more challenged today to monitor my communication skills than I was twenty years ago. Writing this book has increased my commitment to grow in this area even more.

•

Our challenge is to *prove* that what we are saying is valuable.

•

One speaker complained to a group, "I can hardly hear myself speak. For the past ten minutes all I've experienced is noise and interruptions." Then he heard a voice from the back of the room say, "Cheer up, you're not missin' much." Whether we like it or not, our audience is always evaluating whether or not we are worth listening to. Our challenge is to *prove* that what we are saying is valuable.

Listeners aren't always motivated to listen, and on top of that, they often have poor listening habits. We want them to pay attention to what we are saying to them. But let's consider the other side of this subject—how we speak to the listener. Do we speak as though our listeners heard everything we said? Do we continue with our long, abstract lectures and give no opportunities for questions or feedback? Do we talk about issues that influence our relationships without inviting the listener to check out what he has heard?

These are the questions we will consider in this chapter.

Removing Stumbling Blocks to Listening

If I want people to listen to me, I'd better discover what motivates people to listen. It will be valuable to identify some of the bad habits people adopt that makes them poor listeners. For example, we know that *listeners tend to be fickle*. The focus of their attention is liable to change suddenly and unpredictably for a variety of internal and external factors. One moment he may be following our conversation; the next he will be thinking about the exciting basketball game that he watched last night. So knowing that the listener's attention is unstable and apt to flee from our grasp at any second should challenge us to be better communicators. If we don't know how to gain and hold another's interest, it will most likely say "good-bye" without apology.

•

People's readiness
to listen
is significantly
shaped by their
opinion of the
speaker.

•

It's also a fact that people's readiness to listen is significantly shaped by their opinion of the speaker. Imagine yourself ready to attend a lecture on your favorite subject by your favorite speaker. He has not traveled in your vicinity for several years. You tell a work associate of your anticipation, and she says, "I heard him last month in Dallas. He's not the same since he aged. His mind is not as sharp as it was. He doesn't have those colorful illustrations that were so effective. You'll be disappointed." How will your friend's comments influence you? Aren't you likely to be on the lookout for all those failings of which you had been warned?

We also know that listeners build barriers that hinder their receptivity—in chapter 2 we talked about a number of obstacles that block the communication process. Physical, social, emotional, and spiritual barriers can keep a listener from hearing clearly what the speaker wants to share. A speaker may have information that the listener desperately needs, yet listening obstacles may prevent the listener from hearing. We need to know how we can remove some of these barriers or convince a listener that he or she needs to tear them down.

> •
> Poor listening
> is not a barrier that
> is deliberately
> constructed; rather,
> it's a *pattern*
> of relating that
> short-circuits
> communication.
> •

Finally, we know that listeners develop poor listening habits. In some cases, poor listening is not a barrier that is deliberately constructed; rather, it's a *pattern* of relating that short-circuits communication. Trying to listen to a child while reading the newspaper may be one person's bad listening habit; another person may listen to a favorite radio station throughout the day and be distracted from listening to other people.

These barriers stand in the way of accurate, effective communication. Can we do anything about them? Does the speaker have any power to offset such problems? What strategies can we set in place to gain and maintain a listener's attention and interest? The way we answer these questions will determine our effectiveness in gaining the ear of the listener. We need to profit from the counsel of the Book of Proverbs: "A wise man's heart guides his mouth, and his lips promote instruction" (16:23).

A wise person knows how to capture and hold the listener's attention.

Five Powerful Principles

Fortunately we can implement skills which will motivate a person to listen to us. Motivational speakers draw large audiences because they have mastered communication techniques that make listening enjoyable. You can practice these same skills and increase your chances of being heard. They apply whether someone is speaking to fifty thousand people in Shea Stadium, sharing with a small Bible study group, or chatting one-on-one. The following principles can help any speaker gain a hearing:

Begin with your appearance. When we speak, our appearance should complement what we want to say. I know of a well-educated, insightful speaker who was invited to speak at a national gathering of professional youth workers. Though he had valuable information to share, he turned off his listeners and defeated his goal because his appearance didn't draw respect from his listeners. His clothing was "loud" and poorly matched. His tie hung down from his shirt. He didn't appear to be an

•

When we speak, our appearance should complement what we want to say.

•

organized, knowledgeable person, and therefore, his audience tuned him out.

A speaker who dresses in an appropriate manner creates a favorable impression and gains a hearing more easily. I am not suggesting expensive clothing or elaborate dress. Clothing should complement the person wearing it, creating a warm, relaxed picture in the listener's mind. Whenever the listener's attention is distracted by my appearance, I decrease the potential of my communication. My appearance should encourage respect and confidence on the part of the listener.

I am sensitive to the people I'm speaking to. People who attend my home church dress in a very casual manner. When I have an opportunity to preach, I dress in an attractive, yet casual manner that doesn't make me look odd or out of place. But when I am invited to preach at a church where people dress more formally, I put on my suit and tie, so I don't create needless barriers. I know of individuals who seem to feel obligated to create controversy in the way they present themselves. Often their message is lost because the audience is distracted by the person's odd or controversial attire.

> •
> With a little creative thought, a speaker can entice people to listen.
> •

One of our seminary graduates wears a ponytail. He was invited to be a guest speaker at a local church. He called the pastor and told him of his hairstyle to see if it would offend the parishioners. Fortunately, the congregation was open-minded about hairstyles and no problem arose. But my friend was wise to recognize the potential problem it could create.

This issue is also relevant to our family life. When teenagers are frequently among others who dress neatly and attractively, then come home to see Dad slouched in the chair in a dirty undershirt, they will find it more difficult to listen to him with respect.

Use "hooks" to capture attention. With a little creative thought, a speaker can entice people to listen.

My wife described an incident that illustrates this point. She attended an in-service training class for nurses who were updating their nursing skills. At the conclusion of the course the director of personnel at the host hospital was asked to explain employee benefits at the hospital. She began her presentation by sharing a recent newspaper article that outlined the jobs and benefits available to nurses in the 1880s. Winnie commented, "It was an excellent way to get us interested in a potentially dry subject." The personnel director used an effective "hook" to capture the attention of her audience.

Attention-gaining hooks come in many forms. A topic of current interest, a human interest article or story, a thought-provoking question, an eye-catching visual, a humorous exercise—all may be effective attention-getters. Two key characteristics of a good hook are the ability to involve the listener and the appropriateness to the subject matter that follows.

> •
> Two key characteristics of a good hook are the ability to involve the listener and the appropriateness to the subject matter that follows.
> •

For many years I have made it a habit of using hooks in speaking, teaching, and preaching settings. I'd be foolish not to create an inviting opening that says to the listener, "This is worth listening to." A little dose of creative imagination stimulates the listener's curiosity and interest. Not many of us serve cake without putting icing on the top. Why not "ice" our communication to make it attractive and appealing?

Hooks are just as appropriate in one-on-one conversations as in public-speaking situations. Effective speakers use techniques that grab the listener's attention. Sitting in a position that encourages eye contact also invites attention. A good speaker will sit directly across from his listener, so the listener can look into his face.

Speak authoritatively and energetically. The other day I was talking with a friend who applied for a position with the police department in his city. After the written exam was finished, he met for a personal interview. My friend said, "I really blew it. I felt like I was listening to someone other than myself making comments that were disjointed and unclear. If they hire me it will be a miracle from the Lord."

Adequate preparation can do much to gain a listener's respect. When we speak, we would do well to ask ourselves ahead of time, "Am I prepared to gain a hearing? Do I have information gathered which is clear and informative? Could I do some basic research which would tell my listener I have something worth hearing?"

•

Adequate preparation can do much to gain a listener's respect.

•

The manner in which we speak is equally important for keeping an audience's attention. We need to ask ourselves, "Do I convey enthusiasm, excitement, or 'gusto' for my concern? Can others sense that it is important to me? Is my voice level appropriate—loud enough to be heard, but not so loud as to drive my listener away?"

Many of you who are reading this book speak regularly to large and small groups. Do you communicate a presence that makes people want to listen to you? What are those elements which entice the listener with your competence? Think of individuals you enjoy listening to. Jot down on a sheet of paper what voice characteristics and body gestures they use that express their enthusiasm for their subject. Which of these would enrich you as a speaker?

Speak to the listener's interests and needs. Consider this basic principle of communication: people enjoy listening to information that relates to them, their interests, and their needs. A classic example of this is recorded in the Gospel of John. Jesus was weary from a journey from Judea to Galilee. He was resting at a well outside the town of Sychar. A woman approached the well. Normally he would not speak to her because he was a Jew and she was a Samaritan—great hostility existed between the two nationalities. Add to that the fact that men looked down on women and did not speak to them with respect. Yet with only one sentence, Jesus had captured her curiosity, and she recognized that he was not an average Jew. As he addressed her need in a kind and compassionate manner, he gained a captivated listener.

> •
>
> People enjoy listening to information that relates to them, their interests, and their needs.
>
> •

Last week, I was asked to bring a brief devotional message at a family camp held in the mountains outside Colorado Springs. Immediately I thought of the group. One, it would be composed of children, youth, and adults—a wide spectrum of interests. Two, most had traveled all that day and would be weary—interest would wane quickly, so I knew that I needed a "hook" that would involve everyone and the subject matter had to be something that was interesting and relevant to all ages. Finally, I knew that my comments needed to be brief and to the point. I was merely practicing the principles that I am describing to you.

We communicate better when we start with the benefits to the listener—if we have any. Imagine yourself sitting down with your eight-year-old daughter. You want to help her learn to keep her bedroom orderly. How could you approach the topic in a positive way that would help her feel that something good would come from the conversation?

Consider evaluating television commercials for one week. Millions of dollars are spent to appeal to your wants and needs. That money is not spent foolishly. Effective advertisers know how to capture viewers' interests, tap into their sense of wants and needs, and get them to act. What can we learn from their approach about gaining a hearing?

Defuse negative emotions. People listen poorly when they are struggling with intense emotions, especially negative emotions. For example, the individual who is wrestling with feelings of anger will hear less of what we are saying and will filter all of it through his fear filter. The person who feels defensive will be busy checking his emotional walls and gates for any holes. He will be planning what he should say in response to protect himself. He will not listen receptively, positively, or constructively.

> •
> People listen poorly
> when they are
> struggling with
> intense emotions.
> •

Remember the incident of Jesus and the woman at the well? With insight and wisdom, he defused the negative feelings she initially had toward him. He shows us that it can be done quickly and effectively.

You might be asking, "How do I defuse listeners' negative emotions? Don't they own their own emotions?" It is true that individuals are responsible for their own emotions. However, we can do much to create a climate that helps or hinders a listener. Here are two strategies that I use consistently. First, I state my intentions in advance. For example, I may say, "Jean, I need to talk to you about a problem that involves you and me. My intention is to find a solution helpful to both of us, not to embarrass you or put you down." Notice what I'm seeking to communicate. I want Jean to know that I feel positive toward her and that I am not trying to exploit, blame, or humiliate her. I have found this approach helpful in reducing negative feelings in the listener.

The second strategy I use to defuse negative emotions is to avoid "you" statements. "You" statements imply a judgment of the listener and often are accusing, advising, ridiculing, threatening, or demanding. The following are examples:

You never think of anybody but yourself.

[You] get in the house right now.

Your reports are always late.

If you studied more, you wouldn't get failing grades.

I find it helpful to use "I" statements in place of "you" statements. "I" statements focus attention on the feelings the speaker is experiencing, or the concern he or she has. They take the focus off the listener; consequently, he or she is less likely to feel threatened and respond hastily or negatively. The following "I" statements could be used in place of the above "you" statements:

I feel lonely being home by myself every night.

I have supper ready. It's time to come in.

I feel more relaxed when reports are in by five o'clock. Then I have time to record them before I leave.

I'm worried about your failing grades.

These five principles that I've outlined will help you motivate the listener to become involved in what you say. They can increase listenability. For many speakers, these ideas may be new and will require diligence in learning the skills. The benefits, however, are worth the effort.

Now I've Got Them, How Do I Hold Them?

Getting listeners' attention is essential for a good start. But in the long run, you also have to know how to keep their attention. Both are essential to the total communication process. Just as I've given you principles for gaining listener's attention, I want to give you five principles I use to hold their interest. I practice them with my family and friends, as well as when I'm teaching a seminary class, mentoring a student, or speaking at a conference. I honor these principles because I know that they help me get through to my audience.

Eliminate distractions. Listeners can easily be distracted; therefore, a wise speaker removes as many competing influences as possible from the environment. Think of distractions as visual and/or auditory. What will the listener *see* that will distract? Is the television on? Are people walking in and out of the room? Is something moving? What is available that the listener may be tempted to read? These visual distractions may be removed, or you may decide to move to a more suitable location.

> •
> **Listeners can easily be distracted.**
> •

Sounds may also be distracting—a radio, stereo, or television; street noise; and adjoining conversation. Any distracting noise threatens message receptivity; if the message is important, the speaker must consciously reduce the likelihood of outside influences interfering with it. By the way, people vary greatly in their sensitivity to noise. One person may be able to study with the stereo playing, while another will find this very distracting. You may not be bothered by noise from the TV, but it might distract others. Give your listener the benefit of the doubt.

Involve the listener actively. Unfortunately, most public speakers consistently violate this basic principle. Communication is an active, two-way process; the more a listener is involved, the more his or her interest will be maintained. Communication is improved when the speaker thinks in terms of talking *with* the listener rather than talking *at* him.

> •
> The more a listener is involved, the more his or her interest will be maintained.
> •

I recall an extremely frustrating afternoon I spent in the company of a person who talked *at* me the entire time. Although only four of us were present, this one person would talk for long periods of time. The experience was taxing and unprofitable; it was a real temptation not to listen at all!

Here are three skills you can develop to involve listeners in a speaking situation. First, use thought-provoking questions. This forces the listener to participate actively in the communication process. Questions are basic to listener involvement; wise questions can stimulate a listener to think. Even when verbal response is not possible, such as during a speech before a large group, questions keep an audience involved by stimulating the *spirit of inquiry.*

Use statements like:

"Have you ever wondered ____ ?"
"What do you think would happen if ____ ?"
"How would you feel if ____ ?"
"How would you respond if someone asked you ____ ?"

A second method to involve listeners is to *visualize* whenever possible. Whether it takes the form of a simple drawing used in a one-on-one conversation or an overhead projector used before a large audience, a visual keeps a listener's attention by involving his eyes as well as his ears.

I have spoken before large groups for many years. In that time I have made an interesting observation. Whenever I communicate information visually with a projector, I observe a consistent behavior from a significant number of listeners. Ladies begin to rummage through their purses to find paper and pen. Men look in their Bibles to see if they have a piece of paper. Seeing the information incites a desire to write it down. *I rarely see this happen when verbal communication occurs alone.* If there is any way reasonably possible, I communicate visually as well as verbally. I know that my message is getting through more effectively to the listener.

The third way to increase a listener's involvement in a message is to *provide a work sheet* on which the listener can record information that the speaker is giving. Some ministers provide a sermon note sheet for the congregation to use as they preach. My friend Tracee is careful to pass out an agenda sheet when she leads a committee meeting. It keeps the team on track and provides a way for participants to take notes. In situations like these, the listener pays close attention in order to write down what is being said.

•

Well-chosen illustrations tend to personalize the message.

•

Use illustrations. Well-chosen illustrations tend to personalize the message; the listener "sees" it being acted out. If you analyze the messages of your favorite public speakers, you will probably find that they use well-chosen illustrations which allow the listener to see more clearly and vividly the truth or principle being expressed.

Illustrations are valuable in personal conversations as well as in public-speaking situations. Illustrations document our messages and give them credibility; they rescue our comments from being too abstract.

Let's look at an example. A husband says to his wife, "Sweetheart, we need to clean out the pantry closet in the kitchen. I saw bugs on one of the shelves." The wife listens, and the problem is taken care of. Later, the wife tells the husband, "Your saying, 'I saw bugs' helped me know you weren't criticizing me but saw a valid problem."

Here's another example:

Marie: "Ted, I'm concerned that our children are developing bad relations with each other."

Ted: "I don't think there's any problem. They're just kids."

Marie: "Maybe so, but Jody hit Marty three times today, and twice I had to stop an argument."

In both of these examples, the speakers help the listeners by giving specific illustrations—by documenting what they are saying. In this way, they give their partners a clear idea of what they are trying to communicate.

Maintain suspense. Recently I attended a seminar. The speaker was well prepared and obviously knowledgeable about the subject. At the beginning of his presentation, he distributed four pages of notes and then spent the remainder of the lecture going through them. Later, a friend and I shared our responses to the lecture. Both of us said that we had found it much more difficult to be attentive because we had before us all the information the speaker was going to cover. The element of anticipation or surprise was gone.

When information is released progressively instead of all at once, the listener has to keep listening to get the full message. Preachers sometimes violate this principle by giving the major points of their sermons at the beginning. A more effective process would be to give the goal of the message, and then reserve each step toward achieving the goal until its logical place in the presentation.

> •
> When information is released progressively instead of all at once, the listener has to keep listening to get the full message.
> •

Show progress. When I speak or teach, I generally use an overhead or PowerPoint® projector. Frequently people come to me after a lecture or speech and say, "I appreciated your use of visual projection. It helped me follow the progression of your talk. I knew I had not missed any of the essential information." The frequency of this response indicates to me that listeners profit from speaker cues which let them know they are receiving the key points. If anyone has missed information, the speaker's review of the most important issues will point out to him what has been missed.

Time to Reflect and Apply

You can speak so others will listen. If you already do, chances are that you are practicing the essential principles that have been outlined in this chapter. If not, perhaps these ideas will enrich your speaking skills and help you evaluate yourself as a speaker. The following questions have been designed to guide you in applying what you have learned.

1. Checking Up on Yourself

The following items will help you think through the way you communicate. Circle the most appropriate answer.

1.	I recognize that many people have poor listening habits.	Never	Sometimes	Usually
2.	I have specific skills I use to hold the listener's interest.	Never	Sometimes	Usually
3.	I defuse negative emotions when I know they are present.	Never	Sometimes	Usually
4.	I remove as many competing distractions as possible.	Never	Sometimes	Usually
5.	I actively involve the listener when I speak.	Never	Sometimes	Usually
6.	I make use of visual aids when I speak.	Never	Sometimes	Usually
7.	I use illustrations to make my information clear.	Never	Sometimes	Usually
8.	I use suspense to keep the listener actively involved.	Never	Sometimes	Usually

2. Weekly Journaling

Writing out the following ideas will help you process the information from this chapter.

- What speakers' habits turn you off?
- What issues in this chapter challenge you? What specific changes do you want to work on?
- Who could give you helpful feedback on how you speak? When will you talk to this person about this?

3. Going Further

1. Use what has been described in this chapter and develop your own speaker checklist. Jot down the key points that you would look for in an effective speaker.
2. Ask a friend to use this checklist in evaluating your speaking skills. Use the feedback you get from this exercise to find ways that you can become more effective as a speaker.

[Notes]

•

Chapter 1: Help! I'm In over My Head

1. Paul Tournier, *To Understand Each Other* (Philadelphia: Westminster Press, 1966), 26.

2. Lee Iacocca, *Iacocca: An Autobiography* (New York: Bantam, 1984), 54.

3. Good News Broadcaster, May 1981.

4. Sey Chassler, "Help That's Always There," *Parade Magazine,* 31 January 1988, 16.

Chapter 3: Listening with Your Eyes

1. Sherlock Holmes, quoted in Mark Knapp, *Nonverbal Communication in Human Interaction* (New York: Holt, Rinehart & Winston, 1972), 63.

2. Robert Bolton, *People Skills* (Englewood Cliffs, N.J.: Prentice-Hall, 1972), 78.

191

3. Howard Hendricks, *The Seven Laws of the Teacher* (Atlanta: Walk through the Bible Ministries, 1988), 42.

4. Gerald Wilson, Alan Hantz, and Michael Hanna, *Interpersonal Growth through Communication* (Dubuque, Iowa: Wm. C. Brown Publishers, 1992), 287.

Chapter 4: Listening with Your Heart

1. Karl Menninger, quoted in *The Reader's Digest Treasury of Modern Quotations* (New York: Thomas Crowell Co., 1975), 146.

Chapter 6: The Remarkable Question

1. Jesse Nirenberg, *Getting through to People* (Englewood Cliffs, N.J.: Prentice-Hall, 1963), 111.

Chapter 7: Clarifying the Message

1. Ptahhotep, quoted in Lyman Steil et al., *Listening: It Can Change Your Life* (New York: McGraw Hill, 1985).

Chapter 8: Personal Growth through Listening

1. A. W. Tozer, quoted in Warren Wiersbe, ed., *The Best of A. W. Tozer* (Grand Rapids: Baker Book House, 1978), 27.

2. Ibid., 26.

3. Ibid., 20, 21.

Chapter 9: Becoming a Powerful, Perceptive Listener

1. Vance Havner, *Consider Jesus* (Grand Rapids: Baker Books, 1987), 80.

Chapter 10: To Bore or Not to Bore

1. Will Durant, quoted in Lawrence Peter, *Peter's Quotations* (New York: Bantam Books, 1977), 160.

2. Robert Louis Stevenson, quoted in Robert Bastrom, *Listening Behavior* (New York: Guilford Press, 1990), 1.